Ninety And Loving It!

*I had great joy in writing this book.
I hope all who read it will find
some happiness of their own.*

EDNA SAHM

Ninety And Loving It!

*Reflections of an ordinary woman's
extraordinary life*

EDNA SAHM

Creative Living Publications
and
Advantage Community Publishers

Escondido, California

First printing 2008

ISBN 0-9718064-2-X
ATTENTION CORPORATIONS, UNIVERSITIES, COLLEGES AND PROFESSIONAL ORGANIZATIONS: Quantity discounts are available on bulk purchases of this book for educational, gift purposes, or as premiums for increasing magazine subscriptions or renewals. Special books or book excerpts can also be created to fit specific needs.
For information, please contact Creative Living Publications,
306 NW El Norte Parkway, #426, Escondido, CA 92026;
ph 760-741-2762.

TABLE OF CONTENTS

Chapter Five
California Dreaming *37*

Chapter Six
The Love Of My Life *47*

Photo Section 55

Chapter Seven
Into The Limelight *75*

Chapter Eight
The Lands Of My Travels. *83*

Chapter Nine
A Few Words From My Loved Ones *105*

CJ Syztel
Carolyn Gross
Bill Schaul
Arlan

Arnie Arneberg
Arlan, My Son
Escondido Rotary
Larry Lynch
Vivian Doering
Glora Tecca
Jack And Jill Campbell
Linda Bailey
Matthew Midgett
CJ Syztel
Sara Ward
Amy Wandalowski
Linda Courton
Angelo Damante
Tina Inscoe
Joyce Koppelman
Bernie Munn
Irv Erdos
Arlene And Frank Lochridge
California Center For The Arts
Bob And Marilyn Leiter
Raymond A. Sahm

Don't Waste Time
Rich And Poor
Memories Are Great...but Reality Is Better
How Old Are You Today?
Final Thoughts

Foreword

Books have a starting place…how this book began was beyond me. A friend of mine in New York State, Christine Garafola, hooked up with a local professional speaker and author named Carolyn Gross. They met at a conference in San Francisco. Upon hearing that the speaker lived in Escondido California, Christine proudly exclaimed to the speaker, "I know someone in Escondido, the vivacious and wonderful Edna Sahm".

Christine then called me and said, "I think you should meet Carolyn", so we set up a lunch meeting. During this elegant lunch, at one of my many favorite restaurants, I began talking to Carolyn about my adventurous life and how I always wanted to write a book. She looked at me and said, "At ninety years old, what are you waiting for? I think it's about time!"

We left the restaurant and Carolyn had no idea that a fire had been ignited. I started writing on the stories of my life and I couldn't stop. I was writing so much I was missing sleep, some of my writing sessions began at 2:00 am.

In appreciation, I want to thank Carolyn Gross for her confidence in me. I could not have written this book without her expertise, support and help.

I hope you enjoy this compilation of reflections from my lifetime. At ninety and loving it…with joy I bring these bits of life to you!

CHAPTER ONE

A Half-Baked Start to Life

I guess even in the beginning I was in a hurry to enjoy my life. I was born March 6, 1917, on a small farm near Crookston, Minnesota, more than two months early. Outside, a snowstorm beat down on the small country house my parents lived in, howling and snapping at the wooden walls. Inside, Mother Nature was pulling at me as well. Severely premature and only three-and-a-half pounds, I probably shouldn't have even survived the birth.

As I was such a *wee bit of humanity*, and with no hair or fingernails, my parents weren't optimistic I would make it for very long. So my father, wanting to give me a chance at life, turned to my dear grandmother Eugenia and told her, "If you can save her, she's yours." In order to protect me from the harsh cold of a northern Minnesota winter, my grandmother did the only thing she could think of – she placed me into a small box and laid it on the door of an open stove. I stayed there for several weeks, until she felt she could take the chance on my surviving away from the oven's warmth. My sisters would later decide that this is why I'd always seemed so half-baked.

My Mother's Love

Despite the terrible odds, I hung on without any medical care. I remained small, even for a young child, but I was healthy and curious about the world. Once I learned to crawl, I used the opportunity to explore every corner of the farmhouse.

My mother, Rebecca, passed away when I was only three-and-a-half years old. I never really got a chance to know her, and I'm left with only a handful of strong impressions and anecdotes handed down from others. She was born in Montreal, but came across the border to Minnesota as a young woman. Once in the states, she fell in love and married her first husband, Henri. They had a few children together, and seemed to be on the path to a long, normal life together. Unfortunately, poor Henri passed away a few years later, so she married his brother, Edmund, my father. Such unions weren't uncommon in those days, especially in remote, close-knit areas. Together, my parents were scratching out a living by farming the tough northern countryside when I came into the world.

Only eleven months after I was born, Mother gave birth to my sister Irene. Then, not long after, they had a third girl, Esther. Counting the children from her first marriage, Henriette and Armund (my first cousins and three-quarters brother and sister), she now had five young ones. Despite the death of her first husband, my mother had started a new family. With four young daughters and a son, it must have seemed as if she had escaped the troubles that found her so early in life. However, her good fortune was not to last.

A few months after Esther's birth, a devastating influenza pandemic swept the globe, killing tens of thousands of people. I'm not sure how my mother caught it, but I know that the infection took her quickly. Once she became ill, there was little that could be done for her. She simply passed the days in her bedroom growing weaker and weaker until she couldn't hold on any longer.

I can still recall the evening my mother died like it happened yesterday. It was during a howling snowstorm. My father took me up to her room where she laid, covered by a small mountain of blankets. A striking woman of only 28 years reduced to a shivering shadow of herself. I leaned in to give my mother a kiss on the cheek. She bent toward me slightly and smiled, but her skin was cold on my lips. I don't remember much more about her, but that moment has always stayed vivid in my mind. When I saw her and touched her face, I knew she would be leaving us soon. Sadly, I wasn't wrong. Later that night, she slipped out of this world as I'd come into it, in the midst of the wind and cold that swirled bitterly around our house.

The experience of that night left a heavy mark on my childhood. Even though I hadn't really gotten a chance to know my mother, her absence meant that my sisters and I would be cared for by someone else. For a short time, our father's sister looked after us. Strangely, my only recollection was that she didn't particularly take to me, and the feeling was mutual. From that beginning, and all through my childhood, we just didn't seem to agree or see things the same way. This might have created a larger conflict in the home, were it not for my grandmother, Eugenia. With my own mother gone, and my aunt overwhelmed, the task of caring for me fell to her once again.

French Royalty

Eugenia was a fascinating woman. Born in Paris and named for a princess, she certainly had the mindset of a member of royalty. I like to think that whatever stubbornness I inherited, whatever spirit allowed me to hang on in those first few months when I should have faded away, came from her. Once she made a decision, there was simply no moving her from it. Her reliance on the French language was a perfect example. She never once spoke English, even though she understood it perfectly well. She had English-speaking neighbors and read American newspapers, but refused to let the words escape her mouth. I think she simply decided her native language was more elegant, and that was that.

It wasn't only her speech that made Eugenia stubborn. She held onto her other habits just as tightly, like her snuff. Whether it was fashionable or healthy wasn't the point. She enjoyed it, and there wasn't anyone who was going to take it from her. She approached my upbringing with a similar doggedness. As a younger woman, she'd raised eight children of her own, and now she was going to shepherd the next generation if needed. And so she made it her personal mission to be sure that I was fed and clothed.

With her not speaking English, I picked up French as my first language. Unfortunately, I haven't retained it through the years, except to recall the small phrases she would throw out frequently: "C'est la vie!"(That's life), "Oh, mon Dieu!"(Oh, my God), "Bon appetite"(enjoy your meal), and so on. I wish I remembered more, but I do know what I would say to my grandmother if I could see her once more; Merci, ma petite grand'mère!

My grandmother and I went on like this for a couple of years. She would watch over me and try to keep me out of the trouble that I seemed to be drawn to. Mostly they were minor mishaps, like being bitten by a large Saint Bernard or run over by a wagon. Other times, I'd get myself into tougher scrapes, like when I fell into a dam while fishing, or the time I found myself atop a tree I couldn't descend from. No matter what kind of mischief I found, she was always there to pick me up. I'd come to think of my grandmother almost like my real mother, and I think I could have been happy staying with her.

A New Mom and a New Home

Eventually, however, my father remarried to a woman named Adeline. I felt a twinge of fear when I'd heard the news. Even back then, the specter of an unkind stepmother was well-known. What kind of person would she be? What would she think of me? Fortunately, my fears were misplaced. Adeline was a kind stepmother, and I adored her. Despite having two little ones from her first husband, she treated us as if we were her own children as well, giving every ounce of her love to her new family.

Buying the Farm

My father, always wanting to give us the best chance, decided to move the farm from Crookston and got a strip of land over the North Dakota border, close to Grand Forks, where he'd found some work. I wasn't sure what he'd be doing, but I didn't want to ask too many questions, either. Everyone was having trouble making ends meet in those days, and it was no secret that he found occasional work as a "rum runner," smuggling whiskey in from Canada during the prohibition. Despite the stiff penalties he'd face if he got caught, my father kept at it. I think he did it mostly to keep food on the table, although he certainly didn't seem to mind the excitement of it. As nerve-wracking as it must have been, he used to love to tell us how he could "outrun a jackrabbit if it was in the way" when he was trying to escape. He must have been telling the truth, because as poor as we were, we never went hungry and he never went to jail!

We spent a couple of weeks packing up our things, and when we'd finished, he borrowed a team of horses and loaded everything into a wagon. While only a few dozen miles or so on a map, the trip was an arduous one. Following a hard day's travel, we arrived at our new homestead. I suppose the location must have been better, economically speaking, but to me it seemed like a kind of dull purgatory, flat and sloping, in contrast to the trees and hills we'd come to love across the border. The earth stretched out as far as the eye could see, nearly unbothered with trees, hills, or other vertical features. Even so, we were all grateful for the fresh start it represented. And, in the beginning, it seemed as if we were going to get it.

The Voice Box

It wasn't only the scenery that was different. The twenties had arrived, and change was everywhere, even seeping into the quiet Midwestern farming countryside. I can remember when one of the first signs of progress, a working radio, arrived to us in the year 1923.

On a chilly, cloudless evening, we packed into coats and blankets and huddled ourselves together for the walk over to the next farm. Trudging through the snow was a chore, but we were eager to see the "voice box" for ourselves and find out what all the fuss was about.

After an hour, we arrived at the small, rickety farmhouse that lay nearest to our own. We were ushered in toward the fire, even though none of us were concerned about the chill we'd caught from the night. We sat transfixed on the small device in the center of the room.

Our neighbor had constructed the device, and I was skeptical about its value. I wasn't really sure what a radio was or did, but this small wooden box with its array of wires and transistors, didn't look anything special to me. It only worked at night, he said, when the air was still and the signals would carry. What kind of machine needed still air?

He reached over and turned a knob on the small box. Slowly, it came to life. As he slid the tuner from one side to the other, there rose a scratchy, crackling sound, like popcorn at the fair. It was interesting, but I still couldn't figure out what the big deal was. And then, out of nowhere, came the faintest whisper of a voice. You could barely make it out, but it was there, coming from some faraway city and landing in their living room.

I can still recall the odd sensation that stayed with me after hearing that bit of a broadcast. Voices flying through the air…who could imagine such a thing? I had no idea about the kinds of changes that were still to come in my lifetime, but I'd caught a brief glimpse.

In the end, though, I think that the radio made me feel isolated. It stood as a reminder that somewhere, far away from the farm, people were doing exciting things. My thoughts settled in this direction on the long walk home, through drifts of snow and snapping wind. In the black of night, only a few lights burned in the distance – the twinklings of the other farms close to ours. There was no one else around, save for the wolves that watched on from the hills. They never came close, but you could see their eyes shining in the moonlight. Maybe they were hungry or curious. I liked to think that they were watching because we were the same, two families out in the winter night, isolated from the rest of the world.

Joy and Pain

We moved into the farmhouse, and life picked up as normal again – just a farming couple and their large group of kids. We didn't have a lot, but there was always food, and there was always love. In fact, there was enough of it to go around that my father and his new wife had three more children in the span of only a few years.

It was a happy time for me. Even though there were now ten of us for them to look after, there was never a shortage of affection. It seemed that my family had gone through a rough patch and come out the other side. Yet once again, the good times were not to last. My father, who had taken work on construction of a highway across the state, was killed when a piece of equipment fell onto him. I was eight-years-old, and I wondered how we would survive without him.

At first, my stepmother tried to keep us together on the farm. We stayed at home, day after day, living on oatmeal for nearly two months, until we were thin and ragged. There was no money coming into the home, and Adeline was struggling to keep us fed, much less to provide luxuries like new clothes or medicine. I thought back to how my father used to go into town once a year to do our shopping. He would come back with two things. The first was a large bag of flour. We could use it to make bread through the winter, but we had to fight the rats away almost every day. Just like us, they were hungry, so we had to guard every morsel jealously. After we'd used up all the spoonfuls of the powder that we could, we cut the bags into small cloths and towels, as a way to make things go just a bit further.

The second item dad brought was a small bottle (or two) of red wine. Like his mother, my father held steadfastly to his French roots. We usually couldn't afford any milk, but there was almost always red wine on the table. Even at our young ages, my parents would mix it in with water and give us a glass for dinner. They weren't great luxuries, but we had looked forward to them when they came. Now, with my father gone, even the wine and flour had disappeared.

The months wore on, and what little we'd had dwindled to nothing. For the final few weeks, we ate nothing but oatmeal day and night. And then, both obviously and impossibly, we started to run out of that as well. While my siblings and I were too young to worry about the many weights of the world, we all understood that an absence of food was going to be a problem. Between our grumbling stomachs, I could see my stepmother's worry mirrored on the faces around the table each night. Adeline was trying her best, but there was no way to keep up.

In God's Hands

Finally, one morning she told us to put on our best clothes because we were going to church. I'd heard her praying for help before, and thought maybe we were going for that purpose. Still, something told me that this visit wasn't about asking for help from God. She needed to look elsewhere.

When we arrived at the church, an outpost of devout Catholics were perched in the farmlands. I came to another of those defining moments in my life. A man I'll never forget,

Father Klink, told his congregation that the children before them were to be sent to an orphanage the next day. Was there anyone interested in taking a child home and sparing them a life in the institution?

The pause after his offer stretched on like an eternity. I now knew why my stepmother had wept while she dressed us in our Sunday best. She could no longer care for us, and we would be sent away. I looked into the faces spread out through the pews. Some met my gaze, but most turned away. Helping tattered and underfed children was a wonderful cause, but it was the onset of the depression. Most families were having a hard time meeting their own needs. It would be hard to find something for an extra mouth at the table.

Finally, after I'd resigned myself to the orphanage, a middle-aged couple came forward. They looked into my eyes and whispered to the priest. After a few hushed words, he patted them gently on the back. My new foster parents were the Bennetts, a farming couple who lived on a few acres outside of town. They never had any children of their own, and were excited to bring a daughter into their life. My siblings weren't so lucky. After we muttered our tearful goodbyes, they were sent to an orphanage, and I never knew what became of them until many years later.

CHAPTER TWO

Borrowed Love

Life with the Bennetts wasn't perfect, but they gave me all the love you could ask for. They were nearly as poor as my first family had been, surviving mostly by eating what they grew in their own fields. We always had enough to eat, but barely anything more. What they did have, however, was a deep well of love and a pleasant home. They asked me to call them Uncle Matt and Aunt Emily out of respect for my deceased parents, but they cared for me as if I'd been their own. In all the years I lived with them, I never once heard an argument. I'm sure they must have disagreed about something at one time or another, but they had simply decided they were going to be happy and get through things together, and that's exactly what they did. They might not have had money, but I will always be grateful for that gift, the ideal of a peaceful and loving home, they gave me.

The Dust Bowl

The Bennetts certainly weren't alone in their poverty. It wasn't just that the economy was bad. The entire Midwest was a dust bowl, the land stripped bare and laid to powder. Drought had done its job wearing down the vegetation, and then the grasshoppers came in swarms and picked what was left to the bone. During the hot summers, the earth would bake and cause the sky to be listless. Giant clouds of dirty air would take to flight, swirling until they crashed into the side of our home. We would cover the windows and cracks as best we could, but it was impossible to stop the dust particles from filtering in and covering all that we owned with a fine layer. It seemed to be everywhere; on your clothes, in your hair, on your food, and even in your nose and mouth from breathing it in. When I think back to it, I can still taste the grit, and feel the relief that washed over everyone when the rain finally came.

Christmas in July

We didn't have much, but I wasn't new to going without. I'd never known anything different, and it wasn't until I was older that I discovered we were in poverty. I can remember occasionally talking to other children and learning about things like toys and their favorite annual event, Christmas. I had no idea of such a thing. It wasn't that we didn't celebrate the holiday; we just did so without the gifts and fanfare that usually came with the season. The concept seemed foreign to me. What was their favorite time of the year seemed to me a religious observance, nothing more.

On the contrary, my favorite time used to be July. It was a spectacular month, deep into the summer. The harsh winter weather would be long forgotten and still months from its return. My foster parents had decided early on that I was too small to help with farm work, but they would allow me to go outside and assist with the cleaning and painting that came with the warmer season. I relished the opportunity to take in the fresh air and sunshine, wishing it could last all year long. Best of all, in July the fair would come to town. If there were a few nickels left over from the crops, we would all go out and see the bright lights and hear the wonderful sounds. I could even buy a "soda pop," as we called soft drinks then, a luxury that seemed otherworldly.

Polly and Me

My other refuge was to spend time with my horse, Polly. A beautiful dark mare, Polly and I were a lot alike. Both of us had been adopted by the Bennetts, and they had decided that we were each too small to work in the fields. On the warm summer days, we would take long rides through the fields, absorbing the vivid colors of the wildflowers, or the heavy smell of the wheat fields. Sometimes, we'd even be able to make it all the way to the neighbors. They had a couple of children living there, and Polly and I would race against them and their horses. There were no saddles or harnesses, so the only choice was to hold fast and hope not to fall as we blazed through tall grass and sloping ground. I think Polly must have been as stubborn as I was, because we never lost – not even once.

The Curse of Loneliness

Outside of those summer months, however, life on the farm was lonely. Even with loving foster parents, I craved some friends my own age. There were no close neighbors, so I didn't play with many other children. After all the years of poverty, losing my parents and seeing my brother and sisters sent away, I would have given my last breath for a friend.

I was starved for an education as well. After I'd finished grade school, there were no other options available. The closest high school was fourteen miles away. The Bennetts had no way of transporting me there each day, and no money to spend on books or clothes. The only thing that came close was a county library that sat just down the road. Despite my lack of a formal education, I loved taking in books. I would hike down a couple of times a week to visit the small, dusty collection, searching its shelves for anything that might catch my interest. From the old westerns to encyclopedias and biographies, I must have read every volume in that tiny room twice.

God's House

The other defining feature of my life with the Bennetts was their religion. They were as Catholic as my grandmother had been French, and it was something they took very seriously. I can remember how, each fall, Uncle Matt would bring home a barrel of preserved fish, which we'd store outside for dinner each Friday. Even so far out in the country, they insisted on the traditional Catholic supper. While they were a far cry from the lobster and fresh fish I get to enjoy today, it seemed like such a treat to have something different.

Other than the culinary improvement, however, their faith was deep and solemn. They weren't ones to talk about it excessively, but they made sure I understood the tenets of the religion and that we prayed regularly.

I can recall an afternoon around the time I turned thirteen. It was three o'clock on Good Friday, and my foster parents were kneeling for prayer. I was feeling rebellious, and I decided I wasn't going to participate. As they sank to their knees, I stood in the corner and peered out the window. A thunderstorm was brewing outside, and they began their quiet devotionals. I remember thinking I wished that they would just get it over with, so that we could all eat, when suddenly my train of thought was broken. A large bolt of lightning had struck the house and flowed through the telephone. The resulting ball of fire surged out and imposed a pale shock on the room. I was terrified. I later learned that the phenomenon is called St. Elmo's fire, but at the time, it was as if God was personally calling to tell me to shape up and behave. If he was, I certainly got the message. I hit my knees so quickly they were bruised for a week!

The Edge of Life

My quiet life with the Bennetts went as it had for years until I was exposed to tuberculosis when I was fifteen. A farmhand my foster parents had hired came down with the sickness, and I became infected as well. I stayed at home, indoors, for weeks on end while my body fought off the illness. To pass the days, I sat in bed reading stories about far away places. Going through page after page, I decided that if I survived my illness, I would find a way to get out and see the world around me. Over time, I did recover. I'd had a scare, but escaped as healthy as ever. The unfortunate young farmhand was sent off to a sanitarium and died a few weeks later.

Leaving the Nest

While the illness left my body, my desire to see the world did not. I had always felt that the rural Midwest wasn't the place for me, but now that knowledge fused with a strong intention to escape. I loved my foster parents, but I hated the isolation. Worse yet, I seemed to be allergic to the cold that hung over the land for months on end. The wind would snap and bite so hard it caused blisters on my face. The pain they caused was so intense I'd be forced to peel them from my cheeks. Over time, I learned not to leave the house at all during the winter months, unless it was absolutely necessary. Even then, I would cover my body so thoroughly that only my eyes were exposed.

With a pocketful of dreams, when my eighteenth birthday came, I set out into the world. My foster parents and I cried, but they understood that I needed to move on. Their love was more that I could ask for, but I was still lonely. I'd never really had a friend, had never had a boyfriend or even been on a date. There was no future for me to stay for, so I left the tragedies of my childhood behind to find my way as a young woman.

CHAPTER THREE

A Million Miles
Just Up the Road

Although I was eager to escape the Bennett's farm, I didn't have to go that far to get away. From their homestead in Kelly, Grand Forks was only fourteen miles up the road, but it seemed like an eternity of distance. People tend to forget that cars only went about twenty miles an hour in those days, and roads were sparse and winding. As such, the earth seemed to stretch out more in those days, than it does now. Ten or twenty miles of travel felt like fifty or a hundred do now.

Besides, I didn't really have any idea where else I would go. I had no formal education to speak of, and very few friends or contacts. Grand Forks was a larger town, with more chances to find work. My only real prospect was through an acquaintance of mine who had also lived in Kelly, a girl a few years older that I was who I knew from Sunday school. She too, had gone to Grand Forks in search of work, and had found employment as a grocery checker. Through her job, she knew a jeweler who kept a small shop in town. He was blind, and was in search of a nanny to care for his young son.

The Jeweler

Not wanting to waste my one solid chance of finding work, I put on my best dress and caught a ride into town to meet with him. I felt nervous as I strolled into his store filled with gold and jewels, but was relieved when I found him to be very warm and kind. The jeweler, Mr. Daniels, introduced himself and led me to a chair in his shop to explain his situation. He was a gentle man who was very successful and competent professionally, but was somewhat limited by his condition. He relied on his wife to be his eyes in the shop, but that meant no one to care for their son during the day. They simply needed a caretaker to look after the little one. It was a straightforward job, and one I was sure I could handle. The little boy was a treasure, and I fell in love with him right away. With blond hair and big blue eyes, I suppose the only word that you could use for him would be pretty. I was eager to start a new chapter in my life, and hoped I would be chosen.

The interview seemed to go well, but Mr. Daniels said he wanted to know what I looked like before I could take the job. I wasn't sure how this was going to be accomplished, but he simply reached his hands forward and ran them over my face. He had lived a long time without his sight, and must have been used to getting to know people this way. Still, I hadn't been prepared for that kind of question, and I felt nervous that he might think I seemed too young to take care of his boy. Much to my relief, he thought that I had kind features and would be a good fit for his son. I was offered the job, which I gladly accepted.

The Daniels were wealthy people. Living in their home showed me a whole new side to life. They took for granted things I'd never seen or experienced, like an indoor toilet. As a child living with my father, and later with the Bennetts, I had only ever experienced an outhouse.

When you had to use the bathroom, you marched out into a small wooden stall and did your business, using pages from the Sears and Roebuck catalog, if necessary. I know this is difficult to imagine with all the conveniences we have today, but back then, the only time we didn't march outside for the outhouse was when it was too dark or blisteringly cold, and then you used a pot inside.

In the Daniel's home however, you could go whenever you needed, in a comfortable heated space. To be able to use a bathroom seemed like such a luxury! People take such small things for granted, but it was a big deal to me. Having come from such a poor home, everything amazed me, and I think I've carried that feeling with me throughout my life.

Out and About

The position turned out to be a perfect stepping stone. As a nanny, my day was largely confined to the home and my work. But a few times a week, I would have the opportunity to venture out into town. Everything seemed so new and exciting.

Having been on the Bennett's farm most of my life, the shops and people downtown were like a foreign country to me. With every trip, I would see or learn something new, whether it was the latest fashion style, a new book, or a just a different flavor of soda. I didn't have a lot of time or mobility, but my idea of the world was growing larger each and every day.

One of my favorite pastimes was to go to a small Chinese café down the main street. You could get a whole meal for only fifteen cents. Some days, they would serve chop suey which seemed bold and exotic to my inexperienced Midwestern palette. Other times, I would enjoy a pork sandwich accompanied by thick mashed potatoes and a heavy gravy. Again, they were small experiences most people would probably take for granted, but to me, Grand Forks may as well have been Paris.

Center of Attention

It wasn't just the streets and stores that I was learning about either. Socially, I hadn't been exposed to many people outside of my own family, and the few members of the church that frequented. I was just beginning to learn about friends, and especially men. I can remember a Saturday afternoon when the Daniels entered their son into a contest for beautiful children. I figured he'd be a shoe-in. These sorts of spectacles weren't uncommon in the twenties and thirties. Families from the town and the surrounding farms would bring their children to fairs and festivals, where they might compete in races, games, or other activities for colored ribbons.

As we filed into a small meeting hall, the parents told

me to go ahead and walk their son to the stage for his turn. Usually, a child would step up to the front and wave to the audience. From there, the judges would fill out small cards and the youngsters would be applauded.

When his name was called, I stepped forward, holding his hand and leading him to the stage. As he waved, whoops and hollers rained down from the rafters. Men, young and old, were calling and whistling, but I couldn't make out their words. The cheering grew louder, and I couldn't understand why they were clamoring so loudly for the young boy. After a few moments, one of the judges finally whispered in my ear that they weren't cheering for the young man, but for me! I'm not sure if I've ever again been so embarrassed in my life. My face burned a deep shade of crimson, but I managed to carry him offstage. After a couple of minutes had passed, finally they quieted down. I was startled, though. I had no idea how to handle attention from men. I'd only ever met a few boys my own age, and barely even spoken to them. I'd never even come close to a single date. Who knew what it would be like to go on simply one date? I was convinced it was time to find out.

Too Many Suitors

I didn't have to wait long for the perfect opportunity. I had kept in touch with my stepmother Adeline over the years. She was living just outside of Grand Forks where I worked for the Daniels, and every other month she would hold a midnight supper. There would be dozens of people attending, as the suppers served as a kind of social event for the community.

With the nation buried under the depression, many families had them as a way to save money, while still being able to go out. They were a good chance for neighbors to catch up, meet the new people in town, or have a date with someone new without all the pressure of a private setting. As the next midnight supper drew near, a young man nervously asked if I would meet him there. I was a bit taken aback by his bold approach, but said I would love to be escorted. I was ecstatic. I'd never been on a date, and now would be my first chance.

It might have been a wonderful time, except all those years without a boyfriend caught up to me. The following day, another young man from town asked me to go with him. Flattered, I agreed. And then, it happened again. I have no idea what I was thinking, but when all was said and done, I'd agreed to six separate dates for the evening. To this day, I don't know how I imagined I was going to get away with having dinner with half a dozen boys. As the evening drew nearer, though, I couldn't bear to face them. When the night of the midnight supper came, I was so flustered; I went to the small home and hid myself behind a large stove!

A few weeks after the evening's debacle and some embarrassing apologies to make, my social life recovered. I met lots of young men from all walks of life. Some were younger, some were older. Tall and short, rich and poor, I finally got an idea of what it was like to be out in the world meeting different prospective partners. Nothing really came of any of it, but it was such a new sensation to me, getting all this attention.

A Lesson in Heartbreak

After a while, however, I started to get the hang of things and began to get a sense of what I was looking for in a man. I wasn't concerned about money, or the right family. Instead, I knew that I would want someone who would make me feel, in a way, like the Bennetts had. I wanted someone who was full of love and compassion, not full of themselves.

With those priorities in mind, I met the boy who would become the first serious relationship of my young life. His name was Artie Knutson, and he had seen me around town a few times. He was a quiet young man with a terrific smile, and I enjoyed his company. He must have enjoyed mine as well, because we started spending more and more time together.

We'd met in late summer, and during the course of fall and winter we became closer. As the days grew shorter and colder, we found ourselves spending most of our free moments together, not that there were many, as Artie had taken a second job shoveling coal. Times were hard, and I figured he needed the work to keep up on his bills or to provide income for his parents or siblings. Still, when neither of us was working, we'd meet up for a movie or dinner, until finally, we became inseparable. The relationship never felt quite right to me, but I think I was swept away in the excitement of having my first real courtship. Or, maybe I was just so drawn to the fact that he was so drawn to me. I was new to this dimension of the world, and we had seemed to slip into a feeling of togetherness so quickly that to embrace it seemed the natural response.

As spring approached, Artie proposed. I was shocked.

I hadn't known he was so serious, or that he had any way to afford an engagement ring. As it turned out, he'd taken the second job to save for the small diamond band he produced from one knee. Sharing in his excitement, I agreed and slipped it on my finger.

What a terrible mistake that moment was. After the commotion had died down and I had some moments to myself, I was confronted with the stark truth: I loved Artie, but I was not in love with him. I didn't know much about love and marriage, but I knew I couldn't walk down the aisle without being able to commit my whole heart. A couple of days later, Artie came over for a dinner at my stepmother's house. During the course of the meal, I removed the ring from my finger and slipped it into his coat pocket. Without a word, I broke off our engagement. I never saw him again.

Even today, to think of Artie and how our brief engagement played out, causes me a twinge of guilt and pain. He was a very decent young man, and I never meant to cause him any heartache. I guess I was just very naïve. They say time heals all wounds, and I hope that's true. All I can say is that I wish with all of my being that life brought him happiness after we split up, and that he found it in his heart to forgive me.

The Big Screen and the Outside World

On Sundays, Mr. Daniels and his wife would spend the day with their son, so I would have free time to do as I wanted. Most of the time, I would walk down to the movie theater and take in a couple of shows by myself. Back then, I could see two pictures, and then go to a restaurant and have lunch for about a quarter. I loved everything about them, from the drama and romance, to the exotic settings. Still, the movies could only satisfy a small part of my curiosity. I was anxious to get out and see more of the world for myself, and hoped one day I would get a chance.

After a few years, this restlessness got the better of me and I made the difficult decision to move on from Grand Forks. I loved the Daniels, but I still had a feeling of wanderlust. I hadn't seen much of the world, and I wanted to get out and experience more. And so, with dreams of a bigger life, I set off to Minneapolis. While not as large or glamorous as New York or Los Angeles, it was definitely a much bigger city with more to do and more opportunities. That move ended up being a gateway to the rest of my life.

CHAPTER FOUR

You Never Know What's Hidden Behind the Foil

In Minneapolis, I felt like I was finally starting to pull away from the countryside of North Dakota. While the city itself was many times larger than Grand Forks was, I didn't find it difficult to adjust. There were still the same things to do, but there were more ways to do them, and everything was bigger. That suited me just fine. I was entering my twenties, and wanted to see more.

Just as my life was moving on, the world was too. World War II was just beginning in Europe and the Pacific, and the winds of change were everywhere. The depression was ending, and the radio and papers were abuzz with news from overseas. In the United States, society was changing as well. Women were working in all kinds of jobs, and new technologies like telephones, automobiles and airplanes were changing the way we lived.

Happy Hour

Alone in the city, I needed to come up with some way to earn money. I found work at a casino and saloon called 'The Happy Hour.' Dark and smoky, with flashing neon lights casting a pale glow that could never reach its corners, the bar was exactly what you'd picture in a forties hangout. Men would come in after a long week of hard work and throw back a few drinks while trying to gamble their way into some extra money. My task was to walk from table to table, in my cocktail dress, and sell cigarettes.

It wasn't a great job, but it provided a decent income and allowed me the freedom to explore the city during the day. Also, it was a great venue for meeting new friends, something I was still anxious to do after so many years in isolation. I met men and women from all over the country and the world, making acquaintances and venturing out on a few dates here and there. I even met the legendary Bob Hope one night when he was visiting his brother! I had lunches and dinners with all kinds of single young men, from simple waiters and shopkeepers, all the way up to the governor's son. He had pursued me so strongly that I finally relented and went out with him.

A Different Kind of Man

Mostly, though, I found them all to be kind, but not that interesting. There was one man, however, who managed to hold my attention. His name was Arnie, and I'd originally met him many years before, when I was a small girl on the Bennett's farm. One afternoon, my foster parents had taken me to see their sister, who lived just over the state line in Minnesota. A dashing young man had come from the local auto shop to see if they were interested in purchasing a car. Automobiles were new in those days, and he spoke of them so eloquently that an impression of him had been etched in my mind.

Over the years, I ran across him from time to time in Grand Forks, where he had remained in the car business. Now, he had started a tire shop in Minneapolis, and I began to view him differently. A native Norwegian, he was tall with blond hair and striking features. Twenty-three years my elder, he'd come to America long ago and made a life for himself. World War I had arrived when he was only seventeen, and he felt strongly for his new country, so he enlisted and fought for the American side. After it ended, he returned to North Dakota and embraced autos as the way of the future.

In Arnie, I saw the things my other suitors lacked. While he was handsome and relatively well-off, he never felt the need to brag or argue, preferring to keep peaceably to himself. He just had a quiet dignity he carried through his life. In that way, he reminded me of the Bennetts, Uncle Matt and Aunt Emily, with their calm demeanor. I think I was as drawn to his kindhearted nature as I was to his Nordic good looks.

As I would see him in Minneapolis, it became clear he had more than a casual interest in catching up with me. He seemed like a decent man, and I felt intrigued by him. I agreed to go out on a date with him, and fate seemed to take over from there.

The Ferris Wheel of Destiny

On our first date, we went to the fair. It was deep into the summer, and it brought back an enormous flood of memories. I still loved everything about the fair: the magic of it coursing through the lights, the sounds and the smells. As we wandered between booths and rides, we held hands and shared a soda. Finally, we arrived at the main attraction – the Ferris wheel. The view of the skyline was breathtaking, with a warm summer breeze washing over us. Then, as destiny would have it, we got stuck at the very top. For forty-five minutes, we sat talking about our lives and each other with the lights from the fair and the Minneapolis cityscape as a backdrop.

I don't think Arnie could have planned a better first date if he'd tried. After that night, we continued to see each other more frequently, until there was no longer any doubt that we'd be together. After he proposed, we were wed in City Hall, forgoing the traditional church ceremony. It was the beginning of a long and healthy marriage.

Finding My Lost Family

Arnie and I set up house following the ceremony. I continued to work in the casino, first to store away extra cash for our new life together, and then to help support my sister. Not long after our marriage, I started to track down my siblings from the orphanage. I'd never understood why I'd been able to find a home that day in the church when they'd been sent off, but I was hoping to learn that they'd been well. In the back of my mind, I feared they were gone from my life forever. Either way, I wanted to find out what had become of them, and hoped that I'd have the chance to see them again.

One by one, I located them around the areas we'd grown up in. Some were still living in the countryside; others had gone to nearby cities. I sent letters to all of them, hoping to catch up. I was especially pleased to learn that Esther, my youngest and closest sister, was living in Minneapolis. Still so young when she'd been sent to the orphanage, she'd had a hard road along the way, partly due to her fierce determination to be educated. Her love of books and classes had already cost her the kind of normal life I'd been blessed with. She'd bounced from one foster home to another, as each set of foster parents would take her to their home in the country until she discovered that they were too far from school for her to attend. At that point, she would run away from her new life to return to the orphanage. It seemed strange to choose to be an orphan, but I had to admire her will. Esther loved learning, and she wanted an education more than she wanted a family.

Now she was going to nursing school at St. Mary's in Minneapolis. A Catholic academy for young women, it was a rough place to live and learn. The nuns who administrated the facility were ruthless and stern, as many were in those days. Day and night she soldiered on through long shifts – sometimes more than eight hours standing with no rests or bathroom breaks. On her time off, she withstood harsh treatment from her caretakers, designed to bend and beat her into obedience. But she never complained, having chosen her path again and again.

Once we were reunited, I gave her small amounts of money that I could set aside for her to see a movie or get a day away from the school. My original job at the bar had lost its luster when a drunken customer extinguished his cigarette on my thigh. The pain was intense, and I quit that night. My manager, however, didn't want to see me go and offered me a new position. Rather than sell cigarettes, I would offer punchboards, small betting games that could be played for a nickel. On the face of the board would be a series of numbers or letters. Under these was a thin layer of foil, beneath there was a card with a prize, which might be up to fifty dollars (big money in the forties) or nothing at all. I enjoyed the work, but more than that, it afforded me the chance to make extra tips. Occasionally, I could tell from my vantage point which cards were winners. Roughly once a week, I would find someone who was willing to share a prize with me for choosing the correct number. By taking advantage of this small loophole, I was able to support my sister with food and clothes.

What she needed more, however, was moral support. Some evenings, I would sneak into her dormitory through the windows and lie with her in bed. She'd gone nearly her whole life without having anyone hold her, and inside the quiet, sterile walls that were her home, she would weep in my arms.

Branching Out

After we'd been married a few years, Arnie started making some bigger profits from his tire business and my sister finished school, so I quit my job and we started to travel a bit.

We went partly because we wanted to explore the country, but also because Arnie knew that I hated the cold and wanted to get away from it. Even now that I had grown, the harsh snowy winds that blew through Minneapolis caused blisters on my face and buried my mood. Getting away from North Dakota had been an adventure, but I still longed to be in a place where the sky didn't dump snow and ice for half the year.

We drove to the east coast, through New England and down into New York. From there, we explored the south, venturing as far as Florida. I loved the warm weather and the beaches, but it seemed like each time we visited, the coast was wracked with vicious storms. While they weren't snowy, I couldn't imagine living through them every hurricane season.

The west coast seemed more promising. Washington and Oregon impressed me with their lush green forests and snow-capped mountains, but the rain and fog that hung over the land seemed foreboding. On our final trip that way, we nearly returned to Minnesota, but I begged Arnie to take me to California. I'd always heard about its warmth and beauty, and wanted to take it in for myself. He agreed, and we continued south, driving through San Francisco and beyond.

Coming Home

When we arrived in Southern California, I fell in love. It was everything that I'd hoped for: warm, friendly and beautiful. I knew in my heart that we had to make our home there, but wasn't sure how to convince my new husband. Luckily, he had taken to the surroundings as well. Always one for a new adventure, and wanting to please me, he began to arrange for our move.

I'd always told my family and friends that I'd have married the devil himself to get out of the Midwest, but in the end I didn't have to.

CHAPTER FIVE

California Dreaming

To me, Southern California has always been as wonderful in real life as it is in the movies. Where else can you find warm weather, friendly people, and a million things to do on any given day?

After a couple months of looking, Arnie and I found a good situation in Southern California. The warm winters and suburban setting were such a far cry from our life in Minneapolis. I felt both overwhelmed and gratified to be here. Arnie and I were happy with our decision and went about looking for work. We didn't have to look that far. History intervened and brought not only work, but a new America and a new world.

The War Effort

Shortly after we'd arrived in our new state, World War II had set in. Like most Americans, the Japanese attack on Pearl Harbor caught us off guard. When we'd been in Minneapolis, we'd heard of the conflicts overseas, but they seemed so far away. Now, listening to the reports on our crackling radios – we didn't have any televisions – it seemed the fighting was coming home after all.

We hadn't been prepared for a war mindset and it was a little difficult to adjust to. Already in his late fifties, and having already fought his World War, Arnie had found employment working with tires, which were hard to come by during the war. I went back to work as well, finding a job in a machine tool shop. Despite my small frame, I found a job with a Navy contractor. For hours a day, I ran a lathe, stripping down blocks and cylinders of metal into usable parts and tools for the war effort. I made just over ninety dollars a week, which was more than most people earned in those days. At the end of the day, I would smell of grease and metal shavings, but it allowed me to save money for our first home.

As the conflict wore on, I was promoted to management. I started as a machine operator, but now I would be supervising the other men and women working in the plant. Instead of taking the orders, I was giving them! It was definitely a change of pace for me, but I took to it, getting on well with those working above and below me. For the most part, everyone was easy to deal with, and I found that when I needed to, I was able to raise my voice and keep everyone in line. I don't think it's a side of me that many who knew me then would have predicted, or that my friends now would expect, but I held my own on a machine shop floor. I guess big personalities really can trump bigger physiques!

Throughout all of it, we would watch the news to see how

the war was progressing. Some days, we seemed so tantalizingly close to victory. Others, it seemed like the fighting would go on forever. In the weeks before "D- Day," it seemed like everyone – the reporters overseas, the families back at home in America, and even the German soldiers – were waiting for an invasion that was inevitable. What's more, on some level, we all understood that it would be a pivotal moment in history.

When it finally came, on June 6th, 1945, I went to Yosemite Park with my sister, Esther. The trip itself was a bit of an ordeal. Everything was rationed in those days, and Arnie had to install an extra twenty-gallon gas tank in the trunk of our car. In addition, we arranged to fill-up at a friend's station for the return trip. It was so difficult to get anywhere out of town, but we wanted to make it to the park and offer our prayers in a tranquil setting.

We weren't the only ones. Many people, some with relatives overseas, had gathered, wanting a quiet, reflective atmosphere. It was a solemn night. The park officials had not lit the firefall, and we all prayed for our soldiers together. If you've never seen it, the firefall is at the top of Glacier Point where a great bonfire is pushed over the edge of the cliff, appearing to the onlookers below as a glowing waterfall of sparks and fire.

Of course, the Allies were successful and the war did eventually come to an end. And, while I didn't pick up a rifle or fly bombers, I was proud of my contribution to the war effort. Like many women of my time, I was awarded a number of citations and even civilian medals for my part. To me, it really represented a bright moment in American history, with men and women from all walks of life pitching in. It wasn't an easy time, but we all pulled together for the greater good.

Glamour Girl

One night, in the early fifties, Arnie and I decided to go out and take in a picture. It was opening night for this movie, and the whole film industry was out and about town, eager to see how their new creation would fare in the market. We didn't take much notice, except to feel a twinge of excitement. We shared a love of the movies, and it was always wonderful to feel the buzz that comes with a premiere in Los Angeles.

I don't remember much about the feature itself, but after it finished, I was stopped by a man who was also leaving the theater. He stared at me so long, and so intently, I wondered if I knew him from somewhere. His eyes seemed to be lingering on my face, as Mr. Daniels' hands had so long ago, looking for some answer. And, just as I had with the jeweler, I stood dumbstruck, not sure what he was hoping to find.

Finally, he spoke, announcing to me that he was with a film studio. I had a wonderful face, he said, simply wonderful. Would I be interested in meeting him one day for a test shoot?

I was skeptical. Who knew if he was for real, or what he really intended. Seeming to sense my hesitance, he assured me that it would be no more than a few photos, just to see how my face would look in different lighting. Didn't I like movies? Wasn't I interested in being a star?

I had to admit to him that I was. The very thought of it

was dizzying. Could I actually be in movies? I wasn't sure, but this man was the expert, and he assured me again and again that the camera was going to love me.

Whether it would have or not, I'll never know. Not more than a couple of days after our chance meeting, and before our appointment, I got an even bigger bombshell – I was pregnant. In an instant, my fantasies of seeing myself on the big screen were replaced with a new dream of motherhood.

My Greatest Joy

I was ecstatic at the news, but Arnie was shy about wanting anyone to know. Being twenty-three years older than I was, I guess he was embarrassed to have our neighbors know we were expecting. Still, I was happier than I could ever remember. I wasn't sure that I was ever going to get the chance to be a mother, and the knowledge that I would came suddenly and unexpectedly.

In 1947, our son Arlan was born. I can say without a moment's hesitation that he has been the pride and joy of my life. I can still remember lying in the hospital bed, rocking him back and forth and crying tears of joy. I've felt the same way every day since then. What can I say about my son? Over the years, he's become everything that I hoped he would and more. Now sixty years old, he's grown from a wonderful boy into a great and gentle man.

Sweetie Pie

Even as a young boy, Arlan was caring. I remember his first day of school. As I walked him to his classroom, both of our nerves in jangles, we saw some kids tormenting a small cat that had been making its way across the sidewalk. She was a small creature, obviously a stray, with six front toes, a bluish coat and giant eyes that seemed to be begging for help.

Arlan, nearly in tears, pleaded with me to save her. I shooed away the small band of tiny troublemakers that had surrounded the animal and took her in my hands. She was so tiny (I later found out that she could curl up inside a brandy snifter). I turned to my son and told him not to worry, that when he came home, we'd have a new pet. This seemed to brighten him right up, so I tucked the kitty away and sent him to his classes.

When Arlan came home that day, he immediately went for his new pet. After some minor deliberations, he named her 'Sweetie Pie.' He loved her to death, and she loved him right back. In the seventeen years we had her, she never scratched or bit any of us. I guess the moral of the story is, when you give some love, it can come back to you as a lifetime friend.

A Certain Flair

For a short time, I picked up work as an interior designer for a local furniture company. I didn't have any formal training, of course, but the owner had seen me perusing his shop and deduced that I had 'a certain flair' for colors and combinations. It wasn't a long-term career for me, but I did enjoy going into the clients' homes and working with all the different colors and styles that you could mix and match. Best of all, after I was done sampling the myriad of tones and textures together, couples and families would live in my art!

Ordinary Americans

After the war ended and our son was born, Arnie and I lived what could best be described as a normal American life. Most of my close friends who know a bit about me and my life are surprised to hear this. I can't say I blame them; my life has had it share of twists and turns. But for a while, things were quiet for us. A small mobile home park was looking for a manager, and with the personal skills he'd learned over a few decades as an entrepreneur and salesman, Arnie was a natural fit. The park was located in Vista, just north of San Diego. When we arrived, however, it turned out that the park wasn't ready. We'd have to wait another year for the grounds to be ready for residents. Despite the setback, the park in Vista opened with Arnie and me working together to keep an eye on the tenants and the grounds. For more than thirty years, we carried on like people do, settling into a routine of married life – working, starting a family and taking the occasional vacation.

Edna Sahm, Kingmaker

During the sixties and seventies, I became increasingly involved in politics. As a young child, I don't remember having much talk in the home about government or candidates. I knew my foster parents had been devout Irish Catholic Democrats, but then again, most Midwestern farmers were back then. Arnie was a staunch Republican, and I had begun to catch on to his ideals of smaller, conservative government policies.

Even so, I didn't pay much attention to any of it, until our local party chapter decided to put on a membership drive. Mostly it involved getting on the phone, meeting your neighbors, and then asking them if they'd be interested in signing up or attending meetings. I was always one to go and meet new people, whether in person or over the telephone. So the drive sounded like a task that was right up my alley. When it began, I started by making calls and talking to my friends. At first, I only had a couple of people sign up. A small handful of new members was no big deal, but just as when I'd first started dating, I was amazed at the attention I could garner just by reaching out. So, I kept going. At the end of the first segment of the drive, they tallied the new members. The results showed that I brought in the most for our chapter. Still, I kept at it. The drive continued, and after a while, I'd brought in more new faces than anyone else in our county, and then our region. Enjoying the success, I simply kept making calls and asking more people to join. Before I knew it, I'd added 587 people to the party, second-most in California!

As a reward, the party sent me to the 1968 national convention in Phoenix, where I sat next to Barry Goldwater. I couldn't believe that a few telephone conversations had led me to rubbing elbows with political bigwigs.

Looking to duplicate my success, I kept up my efforts to attract new voters and members in the elections that followed. From those first few simple phone calls, I helped to open up five new headquarters, met two presidents, and went to an inauguration. Not bad for just getting out to meet my neighbors!

Taking Our Act Abroad

Other than our political exercises, Arnie and I passed our years by traveling around the world. We both loved seeing new places, and we took every chance that we could to go somewhere different. With each new adventure, I felt more and more like I was finally breaking out of my shell and experiencing all of those faraway places that I had read and dreamed about when I was young. On one trip alone, we saw more than a dozen countries in Europe.

Settling In

When Arnie retired from the tire business, we moved to the Vista mobile home park ourselves. After years of managing the property, it seemed like the perfect place to settle in. We bought a small unit and continued to serve as managers for the properties, collecting rent and seeing to the basic upkeep. As simple as it was, it was a great life. We knew all of our neighbors and everyone got along. I've learned in life that being surrounded by your friends is better than just about anything else you can wish for, and for fouteen years we lived this dream. Eventually, we retired and the property owners sold the park as individual spaces, but I still think fondly of our acquaintances there.

Saying Goodbye

In 1983, Arnie passed away at the age of ninety. I will always think of him as an incredibly kind man who always thought of my happiness. We had a long and joyous marriage, and I wasn't sure what I'd do without him. But, his passing led me to the next stage in my life.

CHAPTER SIX

The Love Of My Life

The greatest thing I've learned in my ninety years is you can never anticipate what will happen next. Life is always full of twists and turns. Just like the surprise ending to a movie, or a secret room in an old house, the world is full of unexpected stories. For many, entering their seventies is a time of winding down into routine and reflection. For me at this milestone, the second part of my life was only gearing up.

New Beginnings

After Arnie passed away, I moved into a small apartment in Escondido. I'd always had an affinity for the town, and I wanted to get away from my former home, stuffed to the brim with its memories. For three years, I worked at putting my life back together. I didn't have much money, but I kept myself busy as best as I could.

One of my hobbies was going down to the local health club for a walk. It helped pass the time, as well as freeing my mind to wander from its familiar trails and into the new places. Over time, I reacquainted myself with the process of opening up to new people and making friends. The months stretched into years, and my circle widened into dozens of men and women from all parts of Escondido. As I had my whole life, I loved making new friends. But there was one, in particular, who changed everything. After a few years at the club, I met my second husband – and the love of my life – Raymond Sahm.

Actually, to be accurate, I should say that I met him again. When my son was a young man, he spent a couple of years at college and decided to enter the working world. His first job was for Raymond, who owned a paint factory in Downey at the time. We'd seen him a couple of times, and he'd always struck me as a nice man, but I didn't really think anything of it at the time.

Dozens of years had gone by, however, and we met at the health club as informal friends. From walking and talking together each day, we were drawn closer to one another. Ray was a widower as well, and we found that we had a lot in common. I enjoyed the way he seemed to look for the good in everything in life, and seemed to bring out the best in me as well. More and more, I started looking forward to our time walking together, and I sensed that he wanted to see more of me as well.

Gravity of Love

Short walks led to long walks, then lunches and dinners. Before long, I knew I wanted to be with him. He was a strong, good-looking man. But more than that, he had the kind of gentle soul that you could look for in five lifetimes and never find. His compassion showed in everything he did. There was simply no room in him for unnecessary anger or bitterness. He looked for the best in every situation, and never wished anyone ill.

The Makings of a Great Man

I could fill another entire book with interesting stories from Ray's life. Ray's father, Henry, had been one of the original founders of Buster Brown shoes, a large outfit in St. Louis. After having been bought out by one of his partners, he decided to head west. He'd contracted tuberculosis, and wanted the mountain air to soothe his lungs. He settled in the high plains of Colorado, already in his forties, and looked to restart his family.

In Boulder, he made a home and met Ray's mother, who would become his third wife. She'd had an interesting journey to Colorado as well. As a young woman in the late 1800's, she'd ventured west in a covered wagon in search of open blue skies and endless prairies. From that storybook backdrop, Ray's parents had six children; three boys and three girls. They would have been a large family on their own, but Ray's father already had eleven children from his first two marriages. Certainly, they must have done something right. All the boys were successful socially and in business. Both of Ray's brothers became fine men, as he was, and all became millionaires in their own right.

Even as one of seventeen children, Raymond was never one to blend into the crowd. Blessed with movie star good looks – he was a dead ringer for the film star Rudolph Valentino – he made all the school girls swoon, even as a youngster.

A Mind like a Diamond

To be fair, he was more than just a pretty face. Ray had a sharp mind, with intellect that cut through complex ideas and situations like a surgeon's knife, a skill that served him well all his life. He'd gone to college to study chemistry, but decided that he'd like to give teaching a try. At Boulder High School, he had taught manual arts, which they call shop class now, for years. For someone with his smarts, it must have seemed like an odd move. But the truth was, Raymond would tell you that he loved teaching. Watching young people discover what was possible, whether it was operating a large machine or finishing their own radio, and then taking that confidence with them in life, granted him an unmatchable sense of joy and accomplishment. Ray cared more about fulfillment than he did about the money, and he got that from teaching.

It wasn't only in the classroom that he enjoyed sharing. When World War II had arrived and I was busy making parts for the Navy, Ray was joining the Air Force as a pilot. By then, he was already in his forties and disqualified from combat duty, but he found a place training new pilots to fly their missions. His patient demeanor and natural skill in the cockpit made him a favorite with his students, who went on to fly missions in Europe, Africa and Asia. It was just his way to be more proud of others for what they'd done, than it was to think of his own triumphs. Even in his final years, we would talk fondly of the young men he helped prepare for the war, and what they'd gone on to accomplish.

The Handsome Capitalist

Just as his love of sharing had drawn him into teaching, however, his curiosity eventually got the best of him. After his teaching career, he searched for a way to put his education in chemistry to good use, and found an unlikely interest in paint. To most people, studying paint would be about as much fun as watching it dry. But where others saw tedium, Raymond saw a challenge. He realized there were better ways to approach the business than had been tried before, and he knew he could make it work. So, without any experience in the industry, Ray moved to California and started a factory. It was only a matter of time before the venture, well-run and producing a strong product, attracted the attention of some larger firms. Noticing his innovative approach to producing paint, not to mention the strong profits it generated, a competitor approached Ray about buying the factory. Never one to miss a good trend, he sold the facility and immediately started another, which he promptly sold again.

After his second factory, Ray grew restless with making paint and decided to go in yet another direction. As a teacher and industrialist, he'd achieved quite a bit. But then, just as I'd found him after so many years, he came upon the intellectual love of his life – investing.

Ray turned his attention to commercial real estate and the stock market. Always a shrewd man, he saw the business angles to coming trends and was able to capitalize on them. He simply had a way of looking at a situation and seeing the likely outcome. In addition to keeping his mind active, he made a lot of money on his investments. Even his advisors were amazed at his ability to size up an investment. By the time we met again, his wealth had risen to the point that what to do with the money was a bigger concern than making more of it.

Wedding Bells

Three months into our courtship, Raymond asked me if I'd like to marry him in Hawaii. It's hard to describe the joy that I felt, except to say that I agreed immediately. With our arrangements in place, we made our reservations and headed to the island like young lovers, full of excitement for our new life together.

Eager to exchange our vows, we departed for the Royal Hawaiian in Oahu. Ray loved the island, as did I, with its crystal blue waters and sandy white beaches. It seemed the perfect setting for our ceremony and everything fell neatly into place until the last minute. Originally, one of Ray's best friends was set to be the best man, but he fell ill and couldn't make it. Searching for a replacement, a thought came to me. I had a friend, Alice Zudy, whom I'd known from all the way back to my days in North Dakota. She moved to Hawaii years before, and we called her to attend. She thought it was a wonderful idea and agreed. But then, incredibly, her husband fell ill as well.

With the wedding hour coming closer, and no best man to stand in, Ray joked that maybe these were bad omens. Beneath his banter, I knew he'd had real reservations. It had not been that long since the passing of his first wife, and he was always one to do the right thing. Looking for some guidance, he'd gone to a see a judge, who had been a longtime friend. The kindly old man listened to his predicament, and then gave some advice that stayed with both of us since. "Life is for the living. Do what you know is right, and live the best lives you can."

Those wise words and his reassuring smile seemed to clear the way for our union. A phone call was made to Sue, my daughter-in-law. She and her family made the trip to Hawaii and stood in our wedding party. The ceremony was gorgeous, held on the grounds of the hotel. When it came time to read my vows, I was so overcome with joy that I could barely manage to speak the words. It was the beginning of the happiest years I've known in my life.

The Marrying Kind

As wonderful as the wedding was, it was only the start. I actually ended up marrying Ray on three different occasions. The first, of course, was in Hawaii, while we were on our impromptu vacation. Soon after, however, we realized that we'd excluded some of our closest acquaintances by having our wedding so far away. So when we'd returned home from the island, we decided to throw another ceremony in our home with friends. Everyone was invited, and nearly everyone came. As thrilled as I'd been to marry Raymond, it was special for me to be able to share it with the other people in our lives.

However, we still weren't done getting married. On our first anniversary, we found ourselves aboard the Pacific Princess, the original love boat. Inside a cathedral of millions of shining stars and a warm summer wind, Captain Theo Apollo presided over a third ceremony.

Of course, these ceremonies were just for us. They didn't make us any more married than we'd been in Hawaii, but I treasured each one. The truth is, I would have married Ray every day if I could have.

More New Family

In addition to Ray, I took to my new family right away. He'd had three stepchildren from his previous marriage, and I was delighted to be a part of their lives. While they were already grown, I remembered the loving way my stepmother, Adeline, had treated me and was determined to show the same love to these grown children as had been extended to me so long ago.

Edna's Place of Birth - March 6, 1917

Edna and Her Siblings
Esther, Henriette, Irene & Armand (left to right, top to bottom)

Edna with Her Two Sisters and Their Husbands

Family &
Friends

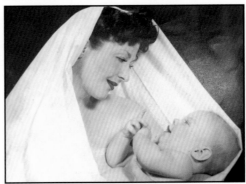
Edna with 3-month Old Arlan

*Arlan's Halloween Costume -
Elvis the "Little" King*

*Family &
Friends*

Arlan Flying His Ultralight

Angelo Damante

Angelo Always Remembers Edna's Birthday

Linda Bailey

Mayor Lori Holt Pfeiler

Irv Erdos

Bernie Munn

Father Jim Rafferty

Bev Riffle

Jack & Jill Campbell

Amy Wandalowski

Matthew Midgett

Gloria Tecca

Vicky Basehore

Joyce Koppelman

*Amy Wandalowski & Linda Bailey
Present Edna with Her First Baby Doll*

Tom Hogarty

*Susie McCormick -
Edna's Daughter-In-Law*

*Arlan & Edna Enjoy the Dedication of Miss Edna's Garden
at the California Center for the Arts, Escondido*

Life with Ray

Ray Sahm at 21 - Looked Like Rudolph Valentino   *A Handsome Couple*

Captain's Cocktail Party Regulars   *Edna & Ray - Cruising Buddies*

Edna & Ray at the Great Wall of China

Haley's Comet Cruise

Best Looking Couple

Edna's Celebrity Friends

Burt Bacharach Hugs Edna

Junior Seau

Doug Flutie

Tim Conway & Harvey Korman Embrace Edna

Miss California, Brittany Hogan

Julio Iglesias Loves Edna

Backstage with Kenny G

Edna & Matthew Midgett with Tippi Hedren

Debbie Reynolds

Rich Little

Edna's Beautiful Garden

Edna's 90th Birthday Party

"Elegant Edna"

Rare Moments

THE ROTARY FOUNDATION OF ROTARY INTERNATIONAL

EDNA SAHM

is hereby named a

PAUL HARRIS FELLOW

in appreciation of tangible and significant assistance given for the furtherance of better understanding and friendly relations among peoples of the world

Edna is proud to be a Paul Harris Fellow and has bestowed this honor on eighteen other individuals.

Edna at the Great Wall of China

Edna Wins the Prize for Best Costume on a Cruise Ship

Grape Day Queen of Escondido

Edna Makes a Special Lei for Father Jim Rafferty

Edna Has a Treat For Her Blue Jay

The Dream Life

For the next ten years, Ray and I lived together happily in the home he'd built in Escondido. Days and weeks passed like a dream. There was never a day when I loved him any less than I had on our wedding day, and I can't recall a time when we ever spoke harshly to each other. He used to call me 'Dolly,' a name he'd given me when we were first wed. That kind of tenderness came through in every word, every meal, every touch that we shared.

When we weren't walking or sharing a meal together, Ray kept investing. Even in his later years, he could spot a strong trend and knew how to capitalize on it. I spent my time cooking, gardening and looking after my new husband. All in all, we simply enjoyed each other and our relaxed life.

A Loss So Deep

My fairytale with Ray, like so many others, ended in tears. It wasn't anger or hostility that took away our time together, but Alzheimer's. After we'd been married for about eight years, my husband started showing symptoms of the illness.

At first, it was gradual. He started forgetting small things like names and appointments. Having had such a sharp mind all his life, it was unlike him to misplace facts, but we didn't give it too much thought. After all, he was nearly ninety, and who didn't lose a bit at that age? Soon, it became apparent that his problems were more severe and he was diagnosed.

Alzheimer's is such a cruel killer, because it takes the mind and not the body. You watch your loved one melt away until they no longer have a sense of themselves or the people who love them. It's such a dark sensation to sit with your husband, your brother, your father – without being recognized.

I can remember one occasion when our friend and financial advisor, Tim, came over to the house. He liked to drop in from time to time just to check up on Ray, who had been a longtime friend and client. After some small talk, Raymond demanded that the man bring a million dollars in cash to the home that afternoon. There was an awkward silence.

Tim finally explained that it was Sunday, and such a transaction wouldn't be possible until banks and businesses reopened. Ray sat and thought about this for a few moments, and then mumbled to himself. I had been busy around the house all morning, tending to my husband and the house. Tim, seeing that my feet were sore and swollen, offered to rub them for me.

Ray jumped up from his chair. "First, you take my money!" he yelled. "Now, you're trying to steal my Dolly!" with that he chased Tim up and out of the house. Tim ran from the back door. I felt horrible, knowing that he had only been trying to be kind. I tried to calm Ray down, when I heard a knock at the front door. Who could that be?

When I opened it, Tim was standing there and said, "Ray it's good to see you. How have you been?" In his illness, Ray had already forgotten the argument. He invited Tim in and they went on to have a lovely visit.

Even in his sickness, however, Raymond remained a loving and gentle man. Rather than become angry and violent, as some with Alzheimer's will, he seemed to crave even more love. Already notorious for his affection, he would steal hugs from everyone around, sometimes dozens a day. Likewise, instead of running from the house, he would sit calmly most of the day.

In his final days, I had help from a local hospice group, who came to our home to help me care for him. From the fine medical care that they provided, to their patient and tender personal treatment, I will never be able to thank them enough for their work. I wanted Ray to be able to live out his days in our home, and it was through their help that this was possible.

The truest thing I could say about Raymond, and the most important, was that he was the finest man I've ever known in my life. After ninety years of life, he never had a single enemy. Loving and gentle, he was the best I could have ever hoped for – the brightest shining example of love to me. My sweet Raymond, I love you and miss you every day!

CHAPTER SEVEN

Into the Limelight

Most of my friends who will read this book know me as the person I am today. I'm sometimes referred to in the media as a philanthropist or a socialite, and while I'm happy to know that people think of me in this way, I also find it a bit ironic. It's a wonderful public persona, but one that hides a lifetime of struggles and joy. It's only in the past decade that I've become such a visible face, starting with the passing of my second husband.

When Raymond died at the age of ninety, I was crushed. It felt like such a weight to wake up without him in our home each morning, with the silence threatening to overpower me each day I was alone. Still, I was determined not to leave. I didn't want to run from our memories; I wanted to hold on to them. I knew right away it would be hard to go on without him, but I didn't just want to waste away my years, cut off from the outside world.

Besides, I'd been left with a substantial amount of money.

For most of my life, the concept of wealth had been foreign to me. Now, I had been entrusted with all of Ray's savings. I knew that he would want me to take it and make a difference.

One of the first things that I did was join the Escondido Women's Club, and then the Escondido Rotary Club. I don't know what I expected to find, but over the past ten years the men and women in these organizations have been like a new family to me. Besides the civic programs that they've put on, they've been a reminder to me of what friendship can mean.

I was 80 years old when I joined, and rather than keep me on the fringes, they've helped me to become more and more involved in the community. For many years now, I've been the official greeter, making sure that anyone who enters their building gets a taste of what we're all about. I'd bet that I've given thousands of hugs and kisses since I've joined, and probably gotten at least as many back.

The social aspect is but a part of what Rotary has done for me. In the same way that they've helped me stay connected through new friends, they also showed me outlets for many of the causes close to my heart. I can't imagine where I would be without Rotary.

Giving is Good

It's ironic that so many of my friends and acquaintances these days know me the way that they do, as a professional donor and public persona. With so many hardships in my early years, this later chapter of my life has so much joy, that all stems from Ray.

When I married him, I knew that he was comfortable, but I had no idea he was wealthy. Put another way, I knew he had money, but I didn't know he had m-o-n-e-y. He never flaunted it or made a big deal out of his wealth, it was simply a luxury that he was pleased to enjoy and share with others.

Ray taught me how to give. Each Christmas, he would stuff envelopes filled with checks to various organizations around town. Some he would deliver himself, but there were too many and he would entrust me to drop off some myself. To give you an idea of how deep his generosity ran, there were so many on the list that it would take me more than a week to finish delivering them all. His philosophy was that Christmas is a time of giving.

He liked to give anonymously, never wanting any credit or recognition for what he'd done. It was a side of him very few people ever saw. Even Ray's own brothers didn't know. I can remember how they thought he was so tight with his checkbook that they used to chide him to give more. He never countered them or said much about it. He simply preferred to work behind the scenes, and never bothered with what anyone thought publicly. Only after his funeral did his family find out about his extensive donations.

What I learned from Ray was that it was about the giving, not the credit. For a while, I followed this philosophy. I tried to continue his tradition of donating money to worthy causes, staying behind the scenes and out of public attention.

After a while, though, I came to realize that at my age it's not worth having to sneak around to do something good. The effort is exhausting. Besides, I don't mind the social functions that keep me active and involved with so many causes. I believe in my heart that he would agree with me that what matters is that some good is done, not how that happens. I only hope that he can be proud of the way I've taken the lessons I learned from him and continued to share with others.

To Truly Give

Probably the most misunderstood aspect of giving and philanthropy is the notion that it's all about money. While it's certainly true that you can help many people when you have deep pockets, that isn't to say that writing a check is the only thing that you can do, or should do.

I believe that with wealth comes responsibility. If you can afford to give to organizations that are doing good in the world, then by all means do it. But if you can't, there are still thousands of other ways to contribute and be involved. Make a phone call and find out how. An hour of your time might not be worth much in a ledger, but it could be priceless to someone else who could use a hand. I promise you that you'll be paid back with friendship and joy that are greater than what you put in.

Philanthropy is a state of mind, not a comma on a bank statement. When you take the chance to give some of your time and effort to another person, or to a cause that is bigger than yourself, you can often make a difference that goes so much further than you could have anticipated.

Local Paparazzi Star

It's a simple rule, I guess: When you give away lots of money, you attract a lot of attention. For the past decade, I've found this to be true. In the beginning, it was small snippets in the paper, noting this donation or that event. From there, things just sort of snowballed until I seemed to know everyone in town.

Once I became so connected, I suppose it was only natural that some of the notoriety came along with it. I remember the first time I read in a paper that someone had referred to me as 'The Queen of Escondido.' I wasn't sure who came up with it, but it seems to have stuck. I've heard variations of it, like 'Mrs. Escondido' and so on in the news. It's hard to know what to make of it. It's certainly gratifying to think that I've made enough of a difference in my community that someone would consider me in that way. On the other hand, it seems like a lot of fuss for doing things that I enjoy.

Somewhere along the way, I guess I decided I would just try to have fun with the whole thing. In the past years, I've gotten to serve as Grape Day Queen (a title which even came with a crown!), the City of Escondido has proclaimed a day for me, I've gotten a bench dedicated at the California Center for the Arts, I've mingled with celebrities, met our political leaders and more. I find it all very flattering, but more than that, it makes me grateful to have so many friends. After living nearly the first twenty years of my life with almost no one to talk to, I'm so thankful to have so many friends in my life.

Grape Day Queen

Our local downtown business association held a contest where any lady who wanted to, could sell tickets to become the Grape Day Queen. It sounded like a kick, so I decided to enter the contest. Before long, many of my friends started buying tickets in bunches, and before I knew it, I'd won! It was a fun time for me. I was given a gorgeous purple gown, and a crown to go with it. I wore them both during a parade that moved through the main streets of Escondido. The whole experience was such a thrill. I got to meet so many new people, and even kept the crown as a souvenir for special occasions. Maybe if I ever meet the Queen of England, we can compare!

Miss California

I haven't just been involved in my own pageants, either. I had the opportunity to meet and help out Brittany Hogan, Miss California. What a lovely girl, the most beautiful I've ever met, inside and out. It was so wonderful to be associated with the pageant, and I'll always have a special place in my heart for her.

Another Milestone

A few months ago, I celebrated my 90th birthday. I'd gotten surprise birthday parties from my friends for the last few years, but this time I wanted to arrange everything myself.

It was a magnificently catered affair with a bit of everything. There were cuts of prime rib, chocolate fountains, and even champagne flutes that glowed different colors from bulbs in the bottom. Everyone had a wonderful time, and it reminded me of how far my life had come compared to what I started with.

I think that the best thing part was that I had more than 160 guests show up. It means everything to me to have so many wonderful people to share my life with. We all ate, drank, and partied the night away. I guess it's possible we overdid it, but how often do you turn 90?

My Garden Kicks Ass

When I'm not busy with my friends or my regular charities, one of my favorite things to do is to spend time in my garden. I have always loved flowers, even back to the days when they grew wild in the fields around our farm. During the summer months, I would wander down to the train tracks that ran through the open fields, searching for the stray roses and tiger lilies that sprung up there. (The only ones that were off limits were the lady slippers, which were the state flower of Minnesota). Even though I hadn't planted them, it felt like the thousands of indigenous varieties that grew and bloomed in the open fields were my private nursery. For those brief few months of warmth, the countryside was awash in color, and I loved it.

In Southern California, of course, I can enjoy flowers all year round. I've taken advantage of this by creating a space that reminds me of the simple floral beauties of my childhood, along with a few extras thrown in. It was even featured in a local tour, where more than a hundred people paid to come see what I'd done.

Besides the dozens of flowers, with their seemingly endless array of shapes and colors, I have a natural rock waterfall, pumped from a reservoir, that runs all day and night. Set aside from the stone pathed area is a row of Hawaiian Plumerias. They're a joy to take care of, starting out very small until they slowly stretch to over twenty feet in height. Even better yet, is when they bloom, I get to make authentic leis for my friends.

The whole garden has a tranquil feel to it. Whenever it seems that life is weighing me down, I just go out for a moment in my garden and take in the peace. I'm hardly ever alone, as the local birds seem to prefer it, as well. I guess we all just love beautiful places.

The Good Life

My life isn't about nonprofit boards or gardening. It's about having my friends and enjoying my days. I never set out to be "known" for any of these wonderful titles, I just wake up in the morning and keep doing the things I want to do.

Most of our lives are such up and down journeys, but I'm so fortunate for the things I have now and know it. In my ninety years, I've seen wealth and poverty, peace and war, good times and bad times. I've had a loving family, found true love, and seen most corners of the world. But most importantly, I've had a great time with all of it.

CHAPTER EIGHT

The Lands of My Travels

If a lack of education has been the one disappointment in my life, then it's been more than made up for by having gotten the opportunity to see so many corners of the globe. From the time I was young, it was my dream to see far-off places. Even the broad streets and shops of Grand Forks seemed like such an adventure. Deep inside, I couldn't shake the yearning to get out and see the larger world. I wanted to take in new countries, with their foreign sights and smells, and experience the vibrant pulse that rises up when there are so many people in the same place.

Shortly after marrying my first husband, Arnie, I finally started to get a chance. He, too, had come from a small town in Norway and wanted to experience more places for himself. Having come to America from Europe, he held a broader view of what lay beyond the horizons. In the beginning, we set out to see different parts of the American countryside. We drove through the Midwest and into the South, venturing as far as the warm, palm-covered coasts of Florida. I took immediately to the warmth, but neither of us was enamored with the frequent storms that seemed to thrash at the peninsula frequently. From there, our journeys took us on short breaks and long weekends to the Northwest, with its pristine beauty, and eventually down into California, where I found my home.

Throughout these trips, however, I couldn't shake the desire to go farther. The drives turned into cruises, crossing oceans instead of interstates, and my love of travel finally matured. From those first two trips with Arnie, to the frequent cruises Ray and I took together, getting out into world beyond our shores has been one of the joys of my life.

Tahiti

One of my first trips overseas was to Tahiti, where I spent an entire month. It was during the sixties, and I was there as a paid traveling companion for my first husband's employer. An elderly man in a wheelchair, it had been his lifelong dream to visit the South Pacific Island, but he was fearful of traveling alone in his condition. This was his final wish that I helped to realize.

Arrnie arranged it that I would accompany him. I don't know what I expected, but when we arrived, the beauty of it literally took my breath away. It was more wonderful than any postcard or beach photo could ever convey. The only word that I can think of is stunning – the one true paradise on earth.

I couldn't believe my luck. There wasn't a great deal that was required of me, outside of assisting my companion with his wheelchair and other small tasks. For more than four weeks, I lounged in paradise taking in wonderful seafood and watching sunsets that seemed to last for hours. The small hotel where we stayed was run by a group of Frenchmen who seemed enamored with the island lifestyle as well. During the day, we'd go for short walks through the long fields of vanilla that grew just beyond the hotel. The smell, sweet and thick, seemed to fill the air until it lived in your nose, your hair and whatever you were wearing. We would also sit on the beach and watch the waves come floating in to gently meet the shore. Then, after the sun retired around nine o'clock, we'd all meet for dinner and drinks.

From Papeete, the capital of Tahiti where we stayed, it was only a short hop to Moorea. Again, the only thing to really be said about this is that it's one of the few places you can go in life that is even better than what is advertised. The island is flooded with unbelievably vivid colors – from the reflective greens of the warm ocean, to the sharp glassy blues of the sky, add to that the white and orange flowers that sprout wild across the landscape.

In Bora Bora, I saw firsthand that the world just below the surface was as teeming with life and variety as the one above. Even the food, mostly seafood creations with a Polynesian twist, wasn't a disappointment, with each dish as fragrant and flavorful as the surrounding hills and jungle. When we weren't feasting on fresh crabs, lobster or papaya, we indulged in pit-roasted pork and even raw fish.

In short, the South Pacific is beautiful beyond description. If you ever want to know what heaven would be like, make it a point to go at least once.

Norway

My first husband Arnie was born in Telemark, a small village in Northern Norway. His family had a long and distinguished history in the area, with one of them having designed several prominent public buildings, and another having been given a rifle by the King of Norway for distinguished service. I think Arnie missed the familiarity of it a bit, so during the sixties, we decided to make the trip to his home. After some initial arrangements were made, he advised some of his family and old friends that we'd be coming. He hadn't seen many of them in several decades, and everyone was excited for the upcoming reunion.

In particular, one of Arnie's childhood friends was so excited to see him again, that he said he would walk into the small village where they'd grown up together to get some kerosene in preparation of our arrival. This wasn't just a stroll down the street. In their village, as with so many parts of the USA at that time, progress was slow in coming, with few cars or other modes of transportation that would make this a less strenuous trip.

Unfortunately, he never reached the town. In preparing so eagerly for our visit, Arnie's friend dropped dead while walking on the way to the kerosene station. Of course, the news was heartbreaking. Instead of going to take in the sights, we attended a funeral and had the loss hanging over our heads for days. Worse yet, when we attended the ceremony, we were seated with the family, facing the mourners. I have never felt so conspicuous, with dozens of the deceased's loved ones staring at us and possibly thinking that we had contributed to his demise.

Years later, I returned to Norway with Raymond, on a cruise that went north, very near to the Arctic Circle. Although cold and austere, I could see why people appreciate Scandinavia for its beauty and wonder. Bundled up and floating through an icy sea, we could look across the bow and peer over to Finland, and Russia just beyond. Even more impressive was the midnight sun, casting its eerie, shallow light down on us nearly constantly. One night, we stayed up to watch it set at 2:15 am, finally leaving the hills in an orange melt of dusk and dawn. The darkness was not long-lived, however, as the sun rose again only fifteen minutes later.

European Tour

On another occasion, Arnie and I went to Europe for a few weeks. There were a lot of places I'd read about in books, and now was my chance to take in the old world capitals and green countryside. The thing about Europe is the history is so close all the time, and so vivid. From the London Bridge to the Coliseum in Rome, most of the things you read about growing up are just out there to see like Vienna, Madrid, Venice – they're all just like the textbooks come to life.

Other places I didn't need a textbook to remember, in particular Germany and France, which brought back memories from my own life during wartime. It's easy to forget that World War II was only a couple of generations ago, with an outcome that is still shaping our world today. I felt a twinge of sadness and rage when I saw the bunker in East Berlin where Hitler ended his life and another time when we went through Checkpoint Charlie to enter Germany. Both were a stark reminder of how the conflict reshaped lives and entire countries.

If you ever want to get a real feel for how our world has become the one we know, then travel abroad. There's no better way to see or understand history than to visit it.

The Love Boat

My very first cruise was on the Pacific Princess, the original love boat. It departed from Acapulco and slid up the coast, making stops in San Diego and Los Angeles. I wasn't sure what to expect, but I fell in love with the whole experience right away. It was hard to believe that you could have delicious food, a couple of drinks and some dancing, all while drifting over the ocean and seeing new places.

Oddly enough, on that maiden cruise we hit some very rough seas. A storm had crept up on the Pacific unexpectedly, throwing the wind and waves into full effect. Our ship, massive as it was, was jostled up and down, right to left. At first, it was a minor inconvenience. But at the rough weather wore on, the movement became even more sudden and severe, causing our captain to close all the kitchen and dining service – it was simply too risky to be handling things like knives and pots of coffee. All around us, people were falling ill, but for whatever reason, Ray and I were immune. Even from that day on, I've never gotten seasick. I guess maybe I really was born to cruise!

Haley's Comet Cruise

In 1986, we went on a cruise that went off the Mexican coast. It was a bit of an unusual trip, because rather than stop at resort towns and tourist stops, the cruise was designed to take us to the best place to view Haley's comet, which travels through the galaxy and returns to earth once every 76 years.

With an astronomer onboard to make sure that we got the best possible viewing, we assembled on the ship's deck at 3 a.m. to look through telescopes and binoculars. There, during the dead hours of the morning, and hundreds of miles into the sea, we saw the comet in all its grandeur. I could see why it was taken as an omen by so many cultures over the centuries. It truly was breathtaking, bright in the sky with a long tail burning behind.

When it was over, we all received t-shirts and had a small party on the deck. But to me, the real highlight was seeing our visitor in space. It was truly magnificent. Unfortunately, it won't be back our way until 2061, so I don't expect to get another chance to see it in person!

The Rock

The Mediterranean is another place that has it all – great weather, incredible food, historic locales, and bright warm shores. Ray and I took a cruise through the sea, and I could see immediately why so many people from around the world flock to its perfect coasts. Like California, it offers a bit of everything.

One of the most interesting sights was the Rock of Gibraltar. You can see it as you enter the Mediterranean south of Spain, jutting out from the deep blue waters. Now maintained by the UK, in ancient Europe it used to be thought of as the limit of the known world; to go over was to risk going down the waterfall that lay just beyond the edge of the map. These days, it's seen in a little less terrifying light. Most of it is a nature preserve, inhabited by wild apes. We were warned as we left the ship to stay away from them, though, as they love to snatch cameras and cause mischief.

Italy

Ask nearly anyone who's never been to Europe where they want to go, and chances are they'll bring up Italy and why not? Besides the incredible pasta dishes, there are hundreds of things to see, and lots of great weather. I first went to Italy with my husband Arnie, and had a great time.

Simply put, it's just a beautiful country. From Rome, to Venice and Naples, it's a land of crooked but scenic roads, and passionate people. One thing that I didn't enjoy, however, was the bravado of the Italian men. Maybe it was just a different time and a different culture, but it seemed like everywhere I went I was getting pinched on the behind, or worse. It was really very rude, although I've heard that their manners have improved since then.

One of my fondest memories was of the Leaning Tower of Pisa, the world's most famous architectural error. It sticks out as a light-hearted reminder of what reality can do to our best intentions. We've all made mistakes, and I could sympathize with the planner. Besides, I saw firsthand for myself how tough the tower can be when I went to take a snapshot and accidentally straightened it out!

Vesuvius

Just a short hop east of Naples lays Mount Vesuvius, the world's most notorious volcano. Its eruption in 79 AD wiped away the small village of Pompeii. This is one of the most well-known and best-documented occurrences in history. Like most people, I'd read the historical accounts, but visiting the ruins cast it differently in my mind.

When the hillside exploded, for the residents of the village, their world ended in an instant. Everyone was frozen and buried as they'd been only moments before. Busy street markets bustling with traders, bath houses filled with the young and old, even chariot races – came crashing to a halt, leaving everyone as a still-frame. This event gave us a reminder that you only get this moment, because the next can be taken from you in an instant.

France

France, of course, is another popular European destination. I've been five times, and love it all, from the quaint countryside to the vibrant urban streets. The art, and especially the paintings in the Loevre, is like none other on earth. Partly, it's because the works themselves are magnificent. But they're made that much better by the fact that they're in the heart of France. This city is so immersed in beauty that it cherishes its treasures and proudly showcases them for visitors. Even the streets themselves, infused with sights and smells of a people who appreciate all that is pleasing, seem to have been arranged as much for aesthetics as function. It's no wonder fashion, cuisine and nearly all of the western arts call it home.

While touring outside of Paris, I was affected heavily by the beaches of Normandy. The government has set the land aside, and you can walk up to the D-Day sites and tread upon the very ground where the Allied troops landed in their famous attack. Beside the shores sit hundreds of rows of crosses, an enormous impromptu cemetery left as a tribute to our dead. Next to them are flags, British and American, to honor the sacrifices of foreign soldiers for France and freedom. For me, the memorial grounds brought back floods of memories from my younger years hearing about the war and working in the machine shop. But even for those who didn't live through the time, I think that the place has a kind of importance that stays with you.

The rest of the nation's history and major sites are spread out, but well worth the journey. The palace at Versailles is an opulent relic from another era. The square where they executed Joan of Arc strikes you with both a calm serenity and a sense of overwhelming history. Old cathedrals stretch your mind into the past and almost drag you into faith with their ancient beauty. The backdrop of green fields and picturesque farming villages charms the soul.

But even though it has its own natural beauty, I think that the scenery of the country takes a back seat to its inhabitants. The French just have a different way of going about things. While the rest of the world worries about work, they are content to share a nice meal and a couple of bottles of wine with friends. What a fantastic way to live! Maybe I just admire them because of my own family roots, remembering my parents and my grandmother, refusing to integrate completely into the American way of life. Either way, I think there are lessons that we could draw from them when it comes to quality of life.

Cuba

In the nineties, I had the opportunity to visit Cuba legally, through the People to People program. I spent ten days on the tiny tropical island, taking in all that is beautiful and exotic from a gorgeous French hotel in downtown Havana.

One of the most intriguing things to see in Cuba was the home of writer Ernest Hemingway. A literary giant, he had always been one of my favorites. I was thrilled to see where he'd lived and composed some of my most beloved books.

Sadly, we weren't able to go inside, but we got a good look through the windows at the various rooms and arrangements. Probably the most notable feature was his extensive library, large even for a man of books. Row after row of dusty volumes crowded their shelves, presumably never to be read again. Otherwise, the grounds were very well cared for; even the dozens of offspring of his famous cats were well fed and groomed as they lounged on the premises.

In terms of weather and scenery, Cuba is as wonderful as any place I've been. Naturally, though, the political problems spill out to affect everything. The people, while incredibly friendly, are very poor. Children go without things like pens and paper. Many in Havana live without decent housing, and those who can afford cars are usually driving very old models that have been kept alive for a lack of available replacements. During our stay, we gave out handfuls of pencils and other small items, but we were left with a helpless, depressed feeling.

Cuba is a beautiful place with kind people. I hope that in the future it will be opened up for more development and tourists, so that it can flourish and join the modern world.

China

I took my first trip to China in 1986. There was no place more foreign or exotic that I'd ever laid my eyes on, or have since. I was awestruck by the sheer scale and history of the nation, which had been formed in ancient times and held together through the centuries. Each temple, square and pagoda seemed to have its own long tale of happenstance, sprinkled with rumors and myths. None was more breathtaking than the Great Wall, which would be a massive achievement even today. Like the pyramids in Giza, it staggers the mind to conceive the work and planning that must have gone into such a creation, given the limited tools and knowledge at hand.

More than anything, however, I was overcome by the cultural differences. Simply put, everything was different... I mean everything. Faces looked different. Cities looked different. The foods, the clothes, the language, even their concept of personal space, were alien to me. For the entire two weeks we were there, I think I was in a constant state of wonderment. Were we still on the same planet?

I returned to China in 2003 with the local Escondido Chamber of Commerce tour. It was amazing to see the difference a couple of decades and a 17-hour flight can make. Upon arriving in Shanghai with its thousands of thirty-story buildings, I could tell immediately how much the country had modernized. I'd been surprised with the quaint, classical Asian architecture the first time around, now I was shocked to see so many new high-rises. Stacked one next to the other, they dominated the horizon even from the air. On the streets, rapid change made itself evident as well. In a stark contrast to the bicycles and round hats I remembered, the main thoroughfares were bustling with cars, buses, vendors and cell phones. It was clear right away that their economy had caught up to the new millennium, bringing with it the good and the bad – computers, cars, smog and the internet had flooded the ancient city.

Change comes to all places, and it's my hope that as the far away lands like China and Africa catch up, the whole world will benefit.

Alaska

What is there to say about Alaska that wouldn't be better expressed in a pictorial? I've been there three times, first in June 1989 on a cruise, then again with Ray a few months later, and finally with my son Arlan. It's the epitome of pristine wilderness beauty. Whether it's the northern latitude or the lack of people, I can't say, but the air seems cleaner and crisper. You can see for so many miles in any direction, the endless sky stretching beneath a pleasant summer sun that hangs above until the early hours of morning.

If you've never been, and want a truly magnificent experience, then I recommend renting a small plane. When I went with my son, we took in the sights through the windows of a small aircraft, and it just seemed to bring it all to life. From Mount McKinley, the highest point in North America, to forests that stretch farther than you can see from miles above, it was like having the whole of it, huge and pristine, reaching out to meet us.

Everything about our 49th state is grand and beautiful. If you haven't been there, make sure you put this on your travel list or you're missing out on the best of the American wilderness.

Ireland

In 2004, I made it to the Emerald Isle. I was accompanying a group that departed from my local Catholic church. After seeing their homeland, it's easy to understand why the Irish are associated with green. The constant rain and temperate climate mean that the whole country is blanketed with moss and overgrowth, giving it a very fresh feeling.

I also got a sense of their overwhelming faith and devotion. As part of a church group, we attended a service nearly every day. Around the chapels we frequented, our attendance was not unique. I admired the locals we saw for their convictions. Their reputation is well deserved. They take their religion very seriously.

The Greek Islands via The Big Apple

In 1985, I went with my daughter-in-law Sue, her husband, and their daughter Janet to the Greek islands. On the way to Europe, we spent three days in New York City, which was my first time ever in the Big Apple. After all these years, and all the places I'd been, I hadn't gotten around to NYC. Of course, if you haven't been to New York, there aren't really words for it, but suffice to say it's an experience that's well worth it.

The Greek Isles themselves are magnificent. Balmy and serene, they seem to be the natural home of the great volumes of art and philosophy that were born there. The only real downside is that most of the ancient streets are narrow and packed, meaning that if you want to get anywhere, you have to walk.

The Mississippi Queen

In the early nineties, Ray and I took a train from Los Angeles and boarded the Mississippi Queen, outbound from

New Orleans. The trip itself took three and a half days. Middle America passed outside our windows and from the deck you could see the dark, muddy gravy that made up this great river while our tug crawled its way through.

We arrived in New Orleans a week before Mardi Gras. The city itself was quite a spectacle, coming off more like a nonstop celebration than a collection of businesses and homes. The whole atmosphere was so festive. You could spend a day around town, seeing crowds of strangers having the best time of their lives, and then go out for wonderful French food and listen to some of the world's best music. What a town!

Of course, I hear much has changed in the last couple of years since Hurricane Katrina hit. But I hope that they're able to rebuild it all. New Orleans is such a wonderful place.

Hawaii

Like Tahiti, Hawaii just seems to stick out like a gem in the sea. I first saw the state in 1965, when I went to visit a friend, Alice Zudy, whom I had known from my early years in North Dakota. Just as I'd moved and gone on to California, she'd settled in Hawaii. It was breathtaking to visit, as Hawaii always is, with its perfect weather, crystal blue waters and white sand beaches.

I returned, of course, for my second wedding with Raymond. That whole experience was so wonderful that it's hard for me to separate my love for Ray with the great time I had there. Those who've been know Hawaii is a magical paradise.

Down Under

Many years ago, Ray and I went to Australia with a group from Escondido. The continent, around the same size as the USA mainland and twice as large as Europe, is something of an enigma. Most of it is engulfed by vast swaths of desert, stretching out over one horizon after another, no matter how you cross it. The coasts, on the other hand, are sparkling and vibrant.

It is this contrast that makes Australia so compelling. The rich variety of settings and creatures you find as the landscape mellows from hot and dry into more temperate zones is truly amazing. Only in a country with both red sandy wastelands and tropical rainforests, could you find the exotic mix that you do there. Kangaroos and koalas roam the bush, while brightly colored talking birds live in the forest. Even the coasts are teeming with unusual inhabitants, from the pearls that grow on the seabed, to the Great Barrier Reef, coloring the ocean floor and drawing thousands of visitors each year.

Best of all, unlike some of the world's wonders, you can experience them close up for yourself. While animals like rhinos and cheetahs need to be viewed from afar, many of Australia's creatures can be seen up close. When we visited, I had the opportunity to hold a koala bear in my own hands. It was just as cute as they always are in magazines, but so bristly. I was a bit past my snorkeling years, but was still tempted to go out into the water and find my way among the tropical fish. Everything was just so accessible. What an experience!

On the same trip, we visited New Zealand, another country

remarkable for its contrasts. Besides the cities, which are much like any other western urban centers, the small island has a bit of everything – sandy beaches, a green, pastured countryside, and even snowcapped mountains. It was as if you'd wrapped up California and Washington State into an area the size of Colorado. We only spent a few days in New Zealand, but I treasure them and would recommend travel here to anyone.

Montreal

In the fall of 1990, Ray and I took a cruise through the Canadian Maritime Provinces. Besides a chance to see a bit more of our northern neighbor, we were excited to take in the famous fall foliage with our own eyes.

We weren't disappointed. One would think that looking at trees might get to be repetitive, but the show they put on was dazzling. It was like moving through a vivid painting. I learned a new appreciation for the hundreds of shades of yellow, orange, red and gold that flowed from one branch to the next, creating a rich tapestry that could only exist in that place. It wasn't just that they were beautiful; it was as if everything about the area – the crisp air, the feeling of the sun creeping down earlier in the day, the subtle scent of maple and oak – enhanced their beauty and made them even better than they would have been on their own.

I got another treat as well that had nothing to do with the scenery. My mother, Rebecca, was born in Montreal, and I started to do some research on the family tree. It turned out that I had several relatives living in the area, and Ray wanted me to have the chance to meet them. He arranged a hotel and a brunch for nearly two dozen of them, so we could become acquainted. After so many years, I got the opportunity to meet some of my cousins and other distant family. It was a fantastic time, and just one more example of how Ray was always such a kind and generous man.

The Caribbean

Raymond used to say that if you hadn't seen the Caribbean, you hadn't lived. After we took a 'Fairwind' Cruise through the islands, I couldn't have agreed more. Obviously, I'm a big fan of tropical places, but there is nothing quite like the beauty of the Caribbean. The sea, which fades from a light, translucent green on the beach to a deep, darkish blue off the shore, is matched only by the almost surreal sunsets, surrounding you in a bath of orange rays for nearly an hour. Even now, it's easy to see why pirates were drawn there. If I had just stolen a mountain of gold, I might try to retire on these pristine beaches too!

Panama

In 1991, I went with friends on a cruise through the Panama Canal. I was left with a pair of opposing conclusions. On the one hand, the construction was an extraordinary achievement. Knowing a bit about the history of the canal, and the struggle that went into constructing it, I can appreciate it as a triumph of engineering and perseverance.

On the other hand, the journey itself was not that

interesting. From the deck of the boat, you could see jungles that seemed deep and thick during the day, dark and foreboding by night. They could have gone back ten miles, or a thousand. You couldn't see much into or through them, so they started to become just a part of the same landscape after a while.

In the last few years, of course, the USA has agreed to turn the canal over to the Panamanians. I don't know if cruises will keep going through the opening and its locks, but to me it was a bit overrated as an experience anyway.

Rio de Janeiro

For anyone thinking of visiting South America, Rio de Janeiro is likely to be one of the first places considered. Like Paris or Tokyo, the city is as much an icon as a destination. With that in mind, Ray and I decided to board the Crown Odyssey, bound for the famous Brazilian metropolis.

The city itself lies perched on the edge of the jungle. During the days spent making our way there, we saw birds and plants of every type. Life seemed to be flowing from the ground, hot and untamed, and into the air. Most spectacular, at least to me, was the plant life. Orchids and rare flowers shot forth from every available corner in exotic strains unknown elsewhere in the world. Trees and bushes pushed themselves out of the ground, both tall and contorted. In several places, their bending expanses almost seemed to create jungle cathedrals, complete with roofs and canopies formed by large draping leaves.

Rio itself was no less wild, if only in an urban way. Again, there was life bustling about in its different ways – some living grandly like the tall trees we'd seen, others clinging on to what could be found and scavenging in the same way the bushes had. Pickpockets and petty thieves flooded the streets, and our cruise group must have seemed like easy prey. Ray and I were not victimized, but many of those in our group had been. A favorite tactic was to have a passerby spill or spray a substance, usually mustard, on some part of your clothing. Moments later, another local would point the stain out to you, and offer to help you clean it off. Naturally, as they would dab the material with one hand, they would help "clean" you-out of your possessions with the other.

In the end, we had a good time in Rio de Janeiro. It was not only scenic, but represented a foray into a different cultural experience. From the ruddy streets, to famous Sugar Loaf Mountain and the statue of Christ the Redeemer on Corcovado Mountain, it was a journey well worth making. But the impression that has always stayed with me was one of poverty and crime. There is certainly a fear for your personal safety and your possessions, but that said, I just felt an overwhelming sadness at the living conditions there. I knew I could try for a thousand lifetimes and never be able to stop their suffering. I certainly know what it's like to be poor, and wish that I could do more to help those people. I think that in my travels I've avoided third-world countries because of that. It's tough to see so many people who could use help.

CHAPTER NINE

A Few Words From My Loved Ones

"My friend Edna lives under a large, beautiful, home-made rainbow that she created partly by putting up with a lot of rain."

--Tom S. Knight

Always Independent

You would think that a 90-year-old would lean on other people in the same way she might lean on a cane. Edna leans on neither. It's not that people don't offer assistance – Edna has many dear friends who are eager to help whenever or wherever she may need it – but it seems she never needs it.

"Can I drive you to the show?" I might ask.

"I'll drive myself!" she'd answer with an unspoken tone that says, "Are you nuts? I can handle it!"

In a way, I almost wish she wouldn't realize how capable

she is, so she would be more inclined to accept a helping hand. After all, a person with a heart like hers deserves a bit of pampering. Whether she's 90 or 19, it's nice to be able to do something for a friend, especially someone like Edna whose life is devoted to helping others.

But, Edna being Edna, she knows exactly how sharp she is. So, the rest of us have to live with the frustration of knowing there's only so much she'll let us do for her. We're OK with that for two reasons: The first is that we take great joy in observing her independence, her energy, and her humanity, and the second is that we know she's aware of how much we love her.

--Irv Erdos

New Friends Always Welcome

The first time I met Edna Sahm was through a pair of mutual friends, Jack & Jill Campbell. They were having a party in their home and invited me along. I had just relocated to Escondido from Anchorage, Alaska, so I knew that I wouldn't know any of the other guests at this party and envisioned a night sitting alone in a corner.

When I arrived, I noticed another guest sitting by herself, at least for the moment. This was surprising, given that she had a very dignified, polished look about her. She gave me an inviting smile, and I sat down next to her. Within minutes, we were chatting as if we were old friends. I thought she was wonderful to talk to, and didn't find out until later that she was THE Edna Sahm, also known as the "First Lady of

Escondido." All I knew was that I was enjoying the evening with someone who has a wonderful sense of humor and an infectious laugh. It was obvious even then, that Edna is an energetic lady who loves life and people.

Before the evening was over, Edna told me about one of her favorite causes, Escondido Rotary. I didn't know then that she was a philanthropist committed to countless charities, just that she seemed very passionate about the group. I was intrigued. Anyone listening to her enthusiasm about Rotary would certainly want to become involved as well. She invited me to a weekly meeting, and I decided to attend.

I should have known that Edna wasn't the type to just show up at a meeting and drink some coffee. When I arrived at Rotary, she was at the door giving welcoming hugs and kisses to arriving members. As soon as she saw me, she took my hand and led me to her table, insisting she wanted me to sit next to her. What's more, Edna sponsored my membership and I have been sitting next to her at Rotary every week since.

I feel extremely fortunate that life has brought us together and made us such great friends. Edna, I love you and I'm very grateful to have you in my life.

-- *Gloria Tecca*

A Pillar of Our Community

I would have to say that I admire Edna's giving spirit most of all. Whether she is handing out plumerias from her garden at a Rotary meeting, or grabbing her checkbook to write out a donation on the spur of the moment for a worthy cause, Edna does everything with a spirit of conviction. She's never afraid to step up to say what she thinks, or to take action if she believes in something. I am thankful for Edna; and the community of Escondido is lucky to have her!

--Tina Inscoe

Don't Give Me Any Grief

When I first met Edna Sahm, she was newly widowed. In the midst of her grief, it would have been understandable if she'd been unfriendly or hard to be around, but she was nothing less than the energetic spirit that we all know and love today.

Since then, she's become a close friend to me and I've been able to witness how truly wonderful she is. There's just no limit to her generosity. She gives so freely of her time and money that it makes me wonder how much the rest of us could do if we just tried to keep up.

I thank God for my friend Edna.

--Vivian Doering

It's Not About the Garden

When Edna asked us to work on her garden, or the 'Bouquet Bank' as it's become known, I knew we were in for a challenge. After all, it wasn't going to be just another grouping of flowers; it would have to be fit for the 'First Lady of Escondido.' As the focal point of her landscape, it's what the public sees when they drive by. I hoped that we'd be able to express her energy and enthusiasm.

I love what we came up with, and I think it mirrors Edna

herself pretty well. It's elegant, but also pleasant on a deeper level. Naturally, it has a lot of solidarity, as well as more than a little flair to it. There are high plants and low plants, some flowering, some green. The individual elements are great, but it's the mixture that makes them special. Come to think of it, I can't think of a better way to describe one of Escondido's greatest and most prominent residents.

--Bill Snapp

Sharing Flowers, Laughs and Life

If you know Edna Sahm, you know she is one of the most inspiring persons you will ever get to meet. If only we could all have her sense of wit, kindness, thoughtfulness, and positive thinking.

I first met Edna many years ago when she and Ray were patients at my husband's dental practice. Even though he has retired, Edna remains a close friend. And who wouldn't want her as a close friend? She's always been so generous – with her time, her friendship, even her flowers. Even years ago, she frequently brought bouquets from her garden to brighten up the dental office. We used to look forward to April and her "spring bloom," which included the deep purple iris, yellow daffodils, and various colors of fragrant roses. Later she included her favorite plumerias and bunches of sweet peas in various pastel shades.

These days, Edna and I are movie buddies. Even when we're just taking in lunch and a film, she seems ready for anything. She usually shows up dressed to the nines in designer clothes and matching jewelry, with a sharp sense of humor to match. Recently, we went to go see a movie that had been given five stars by the reviewers. Half-way through, she turned to me and said with a giggle, "I'm still waiting for the five stars to kick in."

That sense of humor is just one of the things I love so much about her. Every year, we get together on her birthday and I'm always amazed at how well she handles life at every stage. I feel so privileged and honored to have Edna as my friend, my movie buddy, and my mentor.

--*Bernie Blaney*

The Greatest Neighbor

Eight years ago my husband and I purchased a house next door to Edna Sahm. We took it on as a fixer-upper project, and one of the first things we did together was to replace a common dilapidated wooden fence with a beautiful long stucco wall. It didn't take us long to discover what a very special lady we had living next to us. As soon as we started building, Edna voluntarily, unexpectedly and very graciously offered to pay for half the fence. After all she said, this is my fence too!

Edna's taken that giving attitude and applied it to all areas of her life. It's no wonder she's loved by this entire city for all her volunteerism and numerous philanthropic endeavors. It seems no matter where you look, she's doing good. She just doesn't seem to run out of a desire to help. In addition to her dozens of charities, Edna personally volunteered to partner with me on several projects we undertook for St. Clare's Home, a help program for homeless and abused women and children.

I see her zip in and out of her driveway daily, on her way to the numerous clubs and organizations she works with. She is always upbeat, energetic, optimistic, and so full of life! It makes sense that she's always dressed to the nines – beautiful on the inside as well as out. Edna is one classy lady, with a very, very big heart. She is a great neighbor, a wonderful friend, and I love her!

--Arlene Lochridge

Making a Difference, and Looking Good Doing It

There are two things I know about Edna Sahm. The first is that she wants to help the community and feels strongly that her support makes a difference. And she's right, it does! Every community should have an Edna Sahm. She gives and she attends.

The second thing I know is that when I do see her, she is going to look good. She and I find ourselves on stage together once in a while. She usually looks a lot better than I do under the bright lights, and we usually share a good laugh about it. As she says, "Honey, you have to work at it."

--Lori Holt Pfeiler, Mayor of Escondido

Never Afraid to Tell It Like It Is

I am honored to be counted amongst Edna's friends. We've known each other for years, and in that time, she's given me a ton of laughs and some great memories. The thing that

I love about her is, while she may keep having birthdays, she never seems to be getting any older. Sitting next to her each week at Rotary, I get a first-hand view. She doesn't hesitate to moan if someone goes on too long, or to speak up if she agrees or doesn't agree. She's a doodle!

More than anything, though, she is a woman of strong opinions, deep compassion, enormous generosity, and a wonderful sense of humor! I'm glad that she's put her life and advice into print. She certainly tells it like it is!

-- *Jeannie Winton*

A Second Mother

After seven years of friendship, there is only one thing I can really say: I love Edna Sahm!

When I first joined the Escondido Rotary Club, she was the first person to greet me as I arrived each week. Guess what? She still is.

I think the thing that first attracted me to Edna was that she reminded me so much of my own mother, petite yet feisty. Since my mom lived all the way across the country in Florida, Edna was always there for me when I needed someone to stand in. My mother turned 90 last December, and my whole family traveled east to see her. Edna wanted to know everything about the trip, especially seeing what my mom wore to her 90th, as she was planning for the same milestone. Unfortunately, in January, just 6 weeks after that wonderful party, my mom passed away very unexpectedly. Edna has been there for me every minute as I worked through the grief of losing my mother.

Edna is a wonderful mother, and now the only one that I have left. I am so blessed to have had two of the most wonderful caring moms in the world. Not many people can say that.

One of my favorite stories about Edna happened just shortly after I met her. She rode with my husband Randy and me to a Paul Harris Dinner in downtown San Diego. My husband, being the gentleman that he is, asked Edna if he could get her a glass of wine. Edna replied, "No, wine makes my eyes go goofy, but I'll have a double martini." To this day we continue to get her that martini every chance we get.

She is an inspiration for me and so many others. I am proud to be part of her life and I love her with all my heart! But most of all, I am the luckiest person in the world, to have her as my "other mother."

--*Linda Bailey*

An Affair of the Heart

Edna and I are two cards cut from the same deck. I just love her. She's a one of a kind person, someone who just radiates life and energy. There aren't so many times in life that you can say something like that and actually mean it, so I'm overjoyed to have her in my life.

She and I first met at some fundraiser or another. Despite the fact that she's a few decades older than I am – although she might not look it – I felt an immediate spark. We just seemed to understand each other right away, and our friendship has only grown over the years. She's certainly one of the closest people in my life.

For the last ten or twelve years, she's been telling people that she's my girlfriend. What an honor it is to be thought of that way! Besides the fantastic life she's led, the work that she does just goes to show the kind of beautiful, generous person she is inside and out. Whenever we're at events together, I like to remind people that in a different life, she would have been the one for me.

In short, I can only say that I love and adore Edna with all my heart. There isn't anything in her nature or spirit that isn't giving, and how can someone not want to be close to that? I can't imagine what my life would be like without her, and I don't want to.

--Angelo Damante

The Inspiration

Edna reminds me of Ginger Rogers – you know; they say that she did everything Fred Astaire did, only backwards and in high heels.

That's Edna! Because of her, I am not dreading getting old. She is the poster girl for age being a state of mind. "Old" is not a word I ever thought to use to describe her – I'm too busy trying to keep up with her!

I might be happy if I could just pull off the look. Whenever I stop by for a visit, she usually has an elegant outfit hanging on the door. Not only a suit or dress with shoes to match, but even coordinated jewelry! She's always a knockout when she goes out; and she does that nearly every day!

Looking good, I think, is just an outward reflection of

her inner attitude. Edna wakes up every morning and says, "Yes!" She expects each day to be full of joy; if she gets handed something bad, she just takes it and shakes it and makes it into a good day anyway.

I can't think of anyone else, at any age, who has the strength and resilience that Edna has. No wonder she's writing a book in her nineties! I am so proud to be her friend.

--Bev Riffle

A Force of Nature

Edna Sahm is a force of nature. I first met her by using a very time-worn "pick-up" line at a charity event (Edna's natural habitat). I saw this vibrant being across the room, and, walking right up to her, I said, "I want to meet you." My brashness didn't faze our Edna. She graciously replied, "Well, I'd like to meet you, too!" It was one of the luckiest days of my life.

Edna became – and has remained – a caring, supportive, inspirational, and very, very dear friend.

She is a confidant (I know of no one more trustworthy), a skilled raconteur, and a damned good advisor on any subject about which I've ever asked. Edna isn't just decorative – she has good sense.

Beyond her beauty and her guts, perhaps her greatest gift is her warmth. It is genuine, and comes from a heart impossibly bigger than her entire petite body. She is a successful businesswoman, accomplished philanthropist, and loving mother to her son, Arlan.

Edna Sahm has made an entire community better through

her generosity of spirit, and countless lives – mine included – spiritually richer simply by knowing her. I love Edna Sahm!

--Matthew Midgett

A Best Friend and Big Sister

I consider Edna to be not only my best friend, but also a mentor and big sister. She's just a beautiful person, inside and out. It might be a cliché, but that doesn't make it any less true.

Yes, she's a well-known philanthropist, and she does things at 90 that most of us couldn't dream of at 30. But the thing I admire most is the graciousness she's kept through all the trials life has thrown at her. When I met her (at her 84th birthday party), it was in the way most of us know her – as the Edna Sahm we know today. But over the years, as I've gotten filled in on some of her past, it's given me an even greater and deeper respect for who she is.

I can remember an occasion when she came to my home. We were walking through one of the rooms when she stopped cold in her tracks. I couldn't imagine what would have startled her. Before I could ask, I saw that she had tears in her eyes. I followed her gaze over to my doll collection.

As a young girl, she had no toys of any kind – no playthings around the house, no Christmas gifts, no birthday surprises. Her family was simply too poor to afford such luxuries. She recounted how she had once asked her foster parents for a doll, but they, being unable to get one, had given her a toy monkey instead. They had done their best, of course, but she had always wanted a real doll. It was one of the thousands of small hurts she's lived through that never completely heal.

In the years since, I've thrown Edna a surprise birthday party every year (except for her 90th, when she threw a big bash herself.) But for her 89th, I wanted to do something special. So, with the help of Linda Bailey, Edna got the most beautiful doll we could find anywhere. I'll never forget the look on her face or the tears in her eyes when we gave it to her. From time to time, I like to think of that moment, partly for the joy but also as a reminder of how far she's come.

I know it's been a long journey for her, but in the end I couldn't be more proud to be a friend of the person she's become. Edna, I love you!

--Amy Wandalowski

Donor and Friend Extraordinaire

I have worked at the California Center for the Arts, Escondido for the past 15 years. For the first ten I knew Edna as a generous donor, but in name only. Since I've become President of the Center, one of the perks has been to come to know her a person as well. She is a truly beautiful spirit, full of life, with more energy and enthusiasm than many people half her age. It is a genuine blessing to have her as a friend.

--Vicky Basehore

Lifesaver

Edna and I met years ago through a grief group. Through the meetings, I found that we enjoyed each other's company and lived close to one another. Although we were both dealing with personal tragedies, we somehow struck up a friendship that was really more about fun than loss. I think that's a real testament to her personality; her enthusiasm just seems to rub off on everyone.

Lots of people have different reasons for loving Edna – namely her generosity, her sense of humor, or her thousands of other great qualities – but I feel that mine is unique. You see, Edna saved my life.

Over the years, we'd become good friends, usually talking at least once a day on the phone. One Friday afternoon, I fell in my kitchen and broke my arm in three different places. The pain was overwhelming, and I lacked the strength to return to my feet and make it from the house. After lying on the floor for a couple of hours, worrying not only about myself but my small dog who needed to be fed, I heard a familiar sound: the phone ringing for Edna's daily call.

I couldn't make it to the phone to tell her I needed help. I remember staring at the phone and thinking to myself, "Edna, get your butt over here!" Of course, she wouldn't be able to hear me. Edna knew it wouldn't have been unusual for me to be out of the house, and my hopes started to fade. But, as the day turned into the evening, the phone calls continued.

By the next day, my friend became concerned enough to come by my house and check on me. When they saw me on the floor, they called the fire department to break down the door and rescue me. My doctor said later that I wouldn't have survived another night lying there. Thank goodness she came and saved me.

Even if Edna hadn't saved my life, I'd love and treasure her as one of my closest friends. But she did, and I love her all the more for it. Thank you, Edna!

--Joyce Koppelman

We Could All Use More Ednas

Everyone should have a friend like Edna Sahm. I'll never forget the day she called to ask if I'd accompany her to see her friend Joyce. What was the matter, I asked? Edna didn't know, but she hadn't heard from her and was concerned. And really, that's just who she is. We should all be so lucky to have someone care about us like that, and she cares for everyone.

We could all use more Ednas in our lives.

--Jerry Kaufman

More Than a Stepmother

When Edna married Marilyn's father, Raymond, we found out what he already knew: she's a terrific person. It isn't just that she's kind, but that she has a zest for life that can't be kept down. Who else could be as excited about being a mother as she is to go to a presidential inauguration?

We're both so grateful for the happiness she brought our father during the last ten years of his life, and the joy she still brings to ours. From the beginning, she was a wonderful mother to us, as she's been to her own son. It's amazing how much energy she still has after all of these years. We still get together each month, and if we can't make it down to Escondido, she comes to see us!

It's no surprise that she's become so well-known for her generous nature. You just can't keep her down. To us, she became a member of the family right away. Now, she's the only family we have. We love you, Edna!

--Bob & Marilyn Leiter

She Didn't Need Gold to Shine

I can say something that not a lot of Edna's friends can: I knew her when she was poor. The remarkable part is, it's the same woman.

Ray, her second husband, was one of my closest friends, but I actually met Edna long before that. It must have been around 30 years ago. She came into my office, wanting to get started investing. She didn't have much, but we got her started out on something small, just setting aside a few dollars a week. Over the years, I would see her from time to time, as she would stop by my office with a question or just for a quick chat.

At the same time, I used to see Ray frequently. He loved to talk investments, and with his mind, he was a natural. Even if he hadn't been so bright, he would still have been one of my favorite people. He was just a prince of a man – kind and compassionate in a way that's hard for people who didn't know him to understand.

One day, I received a postcard from Ray in the mail. The picture was of a sandy white Hawaiian beach. On the back, he scrawled out a short note saying that he'd run off and gotten married, and that there would be a reception when he returned. I remember thinking that for Ray to have gotten married without even talking to me about it, he must have been very, very sure that he'd chosen the right person. I was eager to see who his new wife was.

When he returned, I went by his house. I still had no idea who he'd married, but when I arrived Edna was in the house. I didn't know that the two even knew each other, but I still didn't put it together. I thought maybe she was arranging the flowers. After all, she always had a flair for style and arrangements, so it made sense in the moment. Imagine my surprise when I found out they'd married each other.

I can remember shortly after the wedding, Edna was worried that her new relatives would think she'd married for money. I knew the idea was ridiculous, but I could understand her concern. Not long after her nuptials, Ray had given her a rather large gift. She never gave it a thought. Rather than hang on to the money, she decided to make it a donation to the California Center for the Arts. I advised Edna to put it away for the future, to take care of herself, but she simply told me that it didn't matter to her. She didn't care about any of that.

Maybe that's what I admire about her the most. For the entire time I've known her, she's held the same passion and views. She's willing to play the public role of philanthropist because she's able to help so many causes that way. But on any given day, she might walk into my office for a chat, and when she does, I know that she's still the same person she's always been. Edna, thanks for being you.

-- Tim Jobe

Do Not Pass Go, Do Not Collect $200

I met Edna several years ago. (It was, and still is, my distinct pleasure and honor to interview prospective members of the Rotary Club of Escondido, as well as integrate them into the club.)

Edna and I hit it off right away. Even at 80 years old, she was so eager to be more involved in the community. I was, and still am, very impressed by her generosity. She doesn't just share her money, but her time as well. It's as if she were driven to stay involved. She's there whenever anyone needs anything, just never seeming to show any signs of slowing down.

There are a lot of great things I could say about her: that she has remarkable instincts about people and situations; that she goes for the gusto like no one else I know; that she seems impossible to intimidate. But I think maybe my favorite quality is that whatever comes into her head also comes out of her mouth immediately, without passing go, and without collecting two hundred dollars. I guess it's part of her charm.

Edna, thanks for everything, and for not being afraid to say what you think or be who you are.

-- *CJ Syztel*

Young at Any Age

The greatest gift I received when I turned 50 was meeting Edna Sahm. Not only does she have a city full of friends, but she has them scattered around the country as well. It was through one of her successful Realtor friends in New York, (the lovely Christine Garafola) that we would meet.

I had no idea what would transpire after our first lunch date, but I watched Edna catch on fire with writing her memoir. Observing her tireless energy, contagious enthusiasm and amazing life story unfold into this book, made me realize that at 50 there is still plenty to anticipate on the good life can bring. To be her facilitator, coach and publisher in making this dream of writing come true, has been an honor. She has already touched so many lives, but now this book will go on and enrich so many more.

Edna, we all want to age like you, we all want to look like you...but mostly, we all want to love like you.

-- Carolyn Gross

"*Ednadido*"

Whether it's a Chamber function, Rotary meeting, charity fundraiser or another community event, it's always nice to see Edna...Sometimes I even get a kiss! If Edna's not there, it's probably not worth attending anyway. She truly is the Queen of Escondido.

When she asked me to help her publish this book, I felt honored to assist her with this endeavor to put together an autobiography that reflects the quality of this lovely lady.

I hope you enjoy reading this book as much as I did.

-- Bill Schaul

A Mother Like No Other

Like many people, I don't remember a lot about my early years, other than to say that we had a happy family. Our home was marked with the normal highs and lows, from chicken pox and removed tonsils to Christmas and summer vacations. No matter what the occasion, however, my mom was always there for me. I remember that she always had a great time getting me ready for Halloween. One year I was a policeman on my little Vespa motorcycle. On another, she gave me guitar lessons so I could go as Elvis. Even back then, her enthusiasm for an occasion was infectious. One year I could have killed her, though. Wanting to outdo her previous work, she decided to dress me up as a bathing beauty, complete with a lady's bathing suit, makeup, falsies, low heels and a perm for my hair. She went all out, and I think I could have died of embarrassment. That's OK Mom, I have forgiven you for that!

I know some of my fondest memories were when she, my father and I would head up to the mountains to camp and cook breakfast over an open fire. I remember one occasion where we decided to go for a short weekend trip to Lake Cachuma. It seemed to be such a long trip and we didn't arrive until after dark. My dad and I had just gotten the tent out when a thunderstorm developed. The wind came up and then the rain and lightning began. Dad and I weren't bothered by the weather, and were about to pitch the tent under a big old oak tree.

There was a problem, though. Mom was not going for any of it. She was convinced that if the lightning didn't get us, then surely the wind was going to push that tree down and kill us all. Inside I thought that even though the wind couldn't, it was possible that her will could! It didn't matter that Dad and I protested; we loaded up and went home. Who was the boss in the Arneberg family? It was, without a doubt, my mother.

At the time, my childhood did not seem like anything unique, except for one detail. For as long as I can recall, my mother was the prettiest of all the mothers in the neighborhood. Actually, she was the prettiest woman I knew, and still is. That alone is kind of remarkable, and I want to thank her for the genes that she passed on to me. I may not feel like I'm a lot to look at, but when I tell people that I am sixty years old they don't believe me, so I guess I must have gotten some of her good traits.

Beyond that though, I know that she loved me as a mother should love her child. And even then, she was always very generous, perhaps a little too generous even, as I got just about everything I wanted. And, like most children, I wanted more than I deserved. I think that's carried over into my adult life. I was talking with a friend just today about my writing this note for her book and I told him as a child I was a spoiled brat. He replied, "You still are!"

Maybe that's not far from the truth. My mother was always a giving woman, and I admire her for that. I know that she's never been shy about giving me her love, or anything else that I needed. I was able to retire at age 50 with the property Ray left me. Without my mother and Ray, I would not be where I am today. Not everyone is nearly as lucky as I have been. I guess I still have a mother who is much more than I deserve.

My mother really is an amazing woman. Even today, having known her all my life, I'm as amazed, as I'm sure are all of you, at how much energy and ambition this woman has. She's just always on the go. She is 90 years old and I am 60. I'm almost ashamed to say that she has more get-up-and-go than I do. This isn't surprising if you know her, but I still find it remarkable.

I want to thank you Mom, for everything. And I want to thank you for just being you.

--Your loving son, Arlan

CHAPTER TEN

Appreciation Pages

I cannot count the number of friends I have, nor can I imagine what my life now would be like without them. One hundred and sixty-one people came to my 90th birthday party. After growing up so lonely, it's such a gift to have them around me. I'd like to say a few words about the people I love and admire so much.

Arnie Arnberg

I used to joke to my friends and family that I'd marry the devil himself to get out of the Midwest, but it turned out I didn't have to. Besides being a handsome, gentle, and loving man, Arnie gave me three things that I'm eternally grateful for – a loving marriage, a life together in California's warmth, and my son, the greatest joy and achievement in my life. Thanks for everything, Arnie. I hope it was a great ride for you, too.

Arlan, My Son

On July 21, 1947, my dream of becoming a mother was

fulfilled. I was so thrilled that I actually used to rock him in my arms and cry. There's not really another way to describe the joy that he's brought me except to say that it can still bring tears to my eyes.

My son has grown from a wonderful boy into a brilliant and amazing man. Now 60 years old, he's definitely still everything I dreamed of. Gentle and resourceful, he has the ability to build anything that he wants. He's a fine son, too, visiting me often, and calling or sending me an e-mail when he can't.

Recently, I was interviewed on television, and the question was posed, "What's the greatest achievement you've ever had in your life?" I didn't even have to think about it. "My son!"

Escondido Rotary

The best way to get a hug is to give one. This I've learned at Rotary, where I've given (and taken) thousands of hugs and kisses. I hope you all know that you've made me the happiest person there. My love to all of you.

Larry Lynch

Larry Lynch was my lifeline to Rotary. Even now, eight years later, I still come to him for his advice and counsel. Larry, you're the greatest!

Vivian Doering

Vivian helped to open a whole other world for me when she sponsored my Rotary membership. I had just lost my husband, Ray, and had a great need at the time. I felt adrift. As a recent widow, she knew how I felt. Thanks for being you, Vivian.

Gloria Tecca

Regardless of what you ask of her, she delivers – whether it's something personal, or to do with Rotary. She was the outstanding person who helped make my 90th birthday party a success. One of my proudest days was when I sponsored her Rotary membership, and now we sit together! I admire her, and am greatly pleased to consider her one of my good friends. Thank you, Gloria Tecca!

Jack and Jill Campbell

Jack and Jill Campbell are two of the world's nicest people. I couldn't tell you which one I love more, so it's a good thing that they're inseparable. Jill is a stellar photographer whose smile and heart are every bit as strong as her eye. And what can I say about Jack? He's absolutely brilliant and the city of Escondido is grateful to have him, both for his intellect and warmth.

Linda Bailey

Linda is a friend who I love dearly and can always count on. She's a busy professional woman with a hectic schedule, and yet, anytime I've ever needed anything, she's never been too busy to help me out. To me, she is the absolute example of what a friend can and should be. I guess that's why she's one of my closest. I love you, Linda Bailey!

Matthew Midgett

Matthew is one of my dearest friends. I adore him, and he knows it. I would hate to have to do without the laughter, creativity and positive energy that he brings to my life. He even arranged for the California Center for the Arts to put up "Miss Edna's Garden" in the corner for my 90th birthday, so that I can be remembered there even after I'm gone. Thank you with all my love, Matthew Midgett!

CJ Syztel

CJ is the life of the Rotary, and someone that I personally admire. She's into anything that's fun and interesting. What would we do without her?

Sara Ward

Sara was our housekeeper and assistant for more than 25 years. In addition to looking after our home, she has been a wonderful friend and caretaker. When Raymond was ill, she looked after both of us. It was a difficult time, and I'm not sure how I would have gotten through it without her.

These days, she doesn't work for me any longer, but we still see each other from time to time as friends. Her daughter drives her by, and we always have hugs for each other. Sara, I want to thank you for all of your help and your friendship.

Amy Wandalowski

Amy has had a trying year, and all I can do is offer my love and friendship. But, she's a fighter, and I know that she'll prevail. We all have so much to thank you for – not only in your work raising funds for charity, but also with your resilient spirit. For that and so much more, I give you my thanks and my love, Amy Wandalowski.

Linda Courton

Often, I wonder how she can do so much, working in the background of our lives and running errands almost nonstop. No matter what needs to be done, she just smiles and does it. Linda Courton, you are a little angel!

Angelo Damante

What can I say about my good friend and admirer? Through the years, he's always been there, and I feel a connection with him that's incredible. Although I love getting flowers and gifts on my birthday and during the twelve days of Christmas, he's never needed an occasion to show his care for me.

I will never find the words to tell him how very much I do think of him and how fortunate I am to have him in my life. Thank you, Angelo Damante.

Tina Inscoe

Tina is one of those people who is an asset to any group, and the California Center for the Arts is lucky to have her. Working away behind the scenes, she's the voice of the organization, opening so many doors with her efforts. Personally, I can't count the number of times that she's fixed a problem or answered a question for me. Love you, Tina!

Joyce Koppelman

Joyce gave me a scare a few years ago. We're good friends who are in the habit of talking to one another daily. One afternoon, I called and didn't get any response. She's so active in the community, always going to lunches and meetings, that I didn't think much of it. But after the second day, I became concerned that she could be in trouble. Jerry Kaufman, from Rotary, agreed to go to her house with me.

When we arrived, we discovered that she had fallen and hurt herself. After a call to the fire department, we were able to enter the house and get her to the hospital. The whole thing reminded me of how wonderful it is to have friends who care for you. I'm so glad to have you in my life, Joyce.

Bernie Munn

Bernie, you've the best decorator in the world. What you did for my 90th birthday party was amazing. The décor of the tables and chairs, the silver and maroon balloons – it was all magnificent. Thank you so much for helping to make my day special.

Irv Erdos

To say that Irv is my favorite photographer would be an understatement. Even though it seems like he's always ready to take my photo – whether I'm smiling or not – he has a method to his madness. Over the years, he's presented me with photos and videos that have made me look better than I've probably deserved.

More than just a skilled shutterbug, Irv is a good friend. I always smile when I know I'm going to see him, simply because he's great to be around. Irv Erdos... I love you and your family!

Arlene and Frank Lochridge

I must have done something right in a past life, because I have the world's best neighbors. Arlene and Frank are wonderful, giving people who seem to be willing to do anything for me. They've made me meals, picked up my mail and newspapers, even been the contact for my security company. Even better, though, is the friendship they bring from their doorstep to mine. Thank you, Lochridges.

California Center for the Arts

I must admit that they are my favorite cause. They do great things for our community's culture and make me feel like "one of the family." Vicky Basehore, the Center's CEO, always has loving words for me, and I look forward to seeing her and that smile. I wish them the greatest success in the decades to come.

Bob and Marilyn Leiter

When I married Raymond Sahm, his children Bob and Marilyn accepted me into their lives and loved me as if I'd been there the whole time. Even now that he's gone, we continue to see each other nearly every month. Each time, they drive several hours just to show me that I'm cared for, and I can't thank them enough for the love they've always shown me. I love you both so much!

Raymond A. Sahm

How do I describe my Raymond? I don't think I can, except to say that he was my life's breath and my soul's delight.

We had ten years together. Eight of them were a pure dream. The other two, living through the hell of Alzheimer's together, were difficult, but it never dampened my love for him. Even in his sickness, he was always a gentleman. I can still see him coming to me with his arms outstretched for a hug ten times a day. I wish I could give him one more.

In our years together, we got to see so many corners of the world. But, I think it was seeing inside of him, to be with such a wonderful person, that was the real journey.

These days, I'm known for the charities I support, and the boards I sit on. But all of that – the money and the giving spirit – I owe to this man who was the love of my life.

It's now almost eleven years since he passed, and I still miss him like it was yesterday. To miss him so much stings my stomach and wells up my eyes.

Ray, I'm looking forward to seeing you again. I love you forever!

CHAPTER ELEVEN

No Formal Education Required

I like the old motto, "Education you get from schools, knowledge you take from the world." I like to hope that this pertains to me, as I certainly feel like it has. When you've been around as long as I have, you figure out a lot of things about the world around you, and life in general. Some are just small tidbits, others are chunks of knowledge or wisdom that I wish I would have come to know many, many decades earlier.

Probably the closest thing I have to regret is that I didn't get more of an education. As a child, I loved reading and learning. But after I was adopted by the Bennetts, grammar school ended and the high school was fourteen miles away. With no car or other reliable means of getting there, the distance meant the end of the line for formal schooling.

Still, even though I was no longer in the classroom, I never stopped being a student. My whole life, I've tried to keep taking in new things, meeting new people, absorbing new ideas. In that process, I've figured out that life is the best teacher anyway. I'd loved to have gone to high school or college, but there are so many things that I've picked up that you can't get off a chalkboard. When you've been all over the world, known and loved so many people, you discover that the facts and the tests that really matter are in your heart, not your head.

Take my advice and let life teach you! Go to school, read great books and learn from the best professors. But no matter what you do, or how much you take in, never stop listening to the lecture that's going on around you all the time. Learn to help others, be open to joy, and fill your days with love. When you've done that, you'll truly be prepared to graduate into the real world.

Don't Waste Time

"Do what you must do today. Tomorrow is promised to no one."

Has there ever been a statement that was more true? In my lifetime, most of my friends and family have come and gone. Some had wonderful lives, others had a hard time. But the one, sure-fire way to leave this world with the fewest regrets is to not put off what you really want to do. Besides, do you really want to take the chance that you'll miss out on your dreams?

No matter what you want to do, it's never too late to start. I'm 90 years old, and just finished my first book. I never had a doubt that I could do it. I only wondered why I waited so long.

Rich and Poor

It's very fashionable for people to say that money doesn't matter. It can't buy you happiness, and the best things in life are free anyway. While I would certainly agree with both of those statements, I think that they're tossed around too easily by those who have never experienced both ends of the spectrum.

I've been rich and I've been poor, and rich is certainly better! No, it won't make you instantly happy, and no, it won't cure all of your problems. Yet I have to admit that things in life seem a bit easier when you don't have to fight mice for scraps of flour.

I would never encourage anyone to live their life for money. There are so many things that are more important – friends, family, and happiness. But, I also get tired of hearing about how important money isn't from people who have always had enough to go around. I've seen both sides and I truly know the difference.

Memories are Great...but Reality is Better

No matter how young or old you are, live your life for today. The past is great, and can be a comforting place, but don't spend too much time there. Greet each day to see what gems are in it.

How Old Are You Today?

If people didn't remind me that I'm 90 years old, I'm not entirely sure I would know. The truth is I don't feel that old. I've lived a long time and seen so many things, but I still wake up each day as excited about the world as I did when I was young.

I think that is the secret to vitality. When it comes to your health, there's a lot of luck involved. There's just no sure way to predict what will happen to you. There's also your diet, lifestyle, and so on. But at the end of the day, I truly believe that how we feel about ourselves and the world around us is such a strong factor in how we live and how long.

Being Edna Sahm is a full time job. Besides my days at Rotary, I stay involved with more than thirty groups that I donate to, and serve on five different boards. Most days, I make time to see at least a few friends, and talk with my son or my sister Irene who still lives in Minnesota with her eight children and thousand or so grandchildren. When I'm not with them, I like to work in my garden, or just go out for a nice meal. I live alone, use my own computer and drive myself anywhere I want to go. I can even get in and out of the bathtub by myself.

There are so many older people who can't do most, or any, of these things. I wish I could share my good fortune with them, but the secret is simple: treat each day like an opened gift, and it just might become one. Hold tight to that attitude – having fun and trying new things – won't just give you a longer life… it will give you a better one.

Final Thoughts

When you hang around as long as I have, you lose so many of your family and friends. In my younger years, it wasn't so hard. After all, even though we love our parents, our aunts and uncles, etc., we know they won't be with us forever. But when loved ones from my generation and younger started to pass, it was more difficult. I used to sometimes feel guilty about this. What right did I have to go on living while my brother, my sisters, my stepchildren, had left this world?

Over time, though, I've learned to accept death for what it is – a part of life. It might be cliché to say, but from my vantage point it's so true. You just don't know what's around the next corner for yourself and those around you. All you can do is have fun today, and hope you'll have another ticket to the fair tomorrow.

It strikes me as odd that so many people are afraid to talk about their death. They seem uncomfortable with the idea of their own demise, and they're surprised when I bring up my own. I've made my plans. I already chose my dress and accessories, and Father Jim Rafferty will officiate at my eulogy at St. Tim's Catholic Church in Escondido.

By the startled faces that I see when I share this, you'd think that I figured out a secret that I wasn't supposed to have. I'll let you in on it: I'm 90 years old and I know I could go at any time. Do they think this is news to me? On the other hand, I wonder if they think they know something I don't. I'm as healthy as I've ever been, so it doesn't seem like my departure is that imminent. Either way, though, I just don't have a fear of it. It comes for all of us. I might make it to 120, or might pass away five minutes after writing this sentence. I'm just going to try to fit in as much life as I can between now and then. Once you stop being afraid to live, you'll probably stop being afraid to die, too.

This journey that we're all on is wonderful. There is fear, and there is pain, but on the balance, I wouldn't have it any other way. I never expected life to turn out so well for me. I am far too grateful to express in words what I feel in my heart. The only thing you can do is enjoy it, and so I do.

GIVE THE GIFT OF
Ninety And Loving It!
TO YOUR FRIENDS AND COLLEAGUES

☐ YES, I want _____ copies of Ninety And Loving It! at $14.95 each, plus $4.95 shipping per book (California residents please add 7.75% sales tax per book).

Canadian orders must be accompanied by a postal money order in U.S. funds. Allow 15 days for delivery.

My check or money order for $_____ is enclosed.

Please charge my: ☐ Visa ☐ MasterCard ☐ Discover ☐ American Express

Name _____

Organization _____

Address _____

City/State/Zip _____

Phone _____ Email _____

Card # _____

Exp. Date _____ Signature _____

Please make your check payable and return to:
Creative Living Publications
306 NW El Norte Parkway, #426 ● Escondido, CA 92026
Call your credit card order to: (760) 741-2762
www.creativelivingpublications.com